MW01031560

Everyday Law in Biblical Israel

Westminster John Knox Press is committed to preserving ancient forests and natural resources. We elected to print this title on 30% post consumer recycled paper, processed chlorine free. As a result, for this printing, we have saved:

5 Trees (40' tall and 6-8" diameter)
2 Million BTUs of Total Energy
454 Pounds of Greenhouse Gases
2,186 Gallons of Wastewater
133 Pounds of Solid Waste

Westminster John Knox Press made this paper choice because our printer, Thomson-Shore, Inc., is a member of Green Press Initiative, a nonprofit program dedicated to supporting authors, publishers, and suppliers in their efforts to reduce their use of fiber obtained from endangered forests.

For more information, visit www.greenpressinitiative.org

Environmental impact estimates were made using the Environmental Defense Paper Calculator. For more information visit: www.edf.org/papercalculator

Everyday Law in Biblical Israel

An Introduction

Raymond Westbrook
Bruce Wells

Westminster John Knox Press
Louisville • Kentucky

© 2009 Raymond Westbrook and Bruce Wells

First edition
Published by Westminster John Knox Press
Louisville, Kentucky

09 10 11 12 13 14 15 16 17 18—10 9 8 7 6 5 4 3 2 1

All rights reserved. No part of this book may be reproduced or transmitted in any form or by any means, electronic or mechanical, including photocopying, recording, or by any information storage or retrieval system, without permission in writing from the publisher. For information, address Westminster John Knox Press, 100 Witherspoon Street, Louisville, Kentucky 40202-1396. Or contact us online at www.wjkbooks.com.

Book design by Sharon Adams
Cover design by Mark Abrams
Cover art: Reconstruction of Solomon's Palace, Solomon's Temple, Jerusalem.
Photo © DeA Picture Library /Art Resource, NY.

Library of Congress Cataloging-in-Publication Data

Westbrook, Raymond.
Everyday law in biblical Israel : an introduction / Raymond Westbrook and Bruce Wells.
p. cm.
Includes bibliographical references and index.
ISBN 978-0-664-23497-3 (alk. paper)
1. Mishpat Ivri—History—To 1500. 2. Bible. O.T.—Criticism, interpretation, etc.
I. Wells, Bruce. II. Title.
BM520.52.W47 2009
340.5'8—dc22

2009006575

PRINTED IN THE UNITED STATES OF AMERICA

♾ The paper used in this book meets the minimum requirements of the American National Standard for Information Sciences—Permanence of Paper for Printed Library Materials, ANSI Z39.48-1992.

Westminster John Knox Press advocates the responsible use of our natural resources. The text paper of this book is made from 30% postconsumer waste.

Contents

After a prolonged bout with cancer, my teacher, mentor, colleague, and friend, Raymond Westbrook, passed away while this book was in press. His commitment to scholarship and his courage and grace during the last months of his life were a powerful inspiration to all who knew him.

—Bruce Wells

In memory of
Raymond Westbrook
1946–2009

Abbreviations of Cuneiform Law Codes

HL	Hittite Laws
LE	Laws of Eshnunna
LH	Laws of Hammurabi
LL	Laws of Lipit-Ishtar
LU	Laws of Ur-Namma
MAL	Middle Assyrian Laws
NBL	Neo-Babylonian Laws

Time Line and Sources

3000	MESOPOTAMIA	ANATOLIA & MEDITERRANEAN	EGYPT	PERIOD
	Old Sumerian/ Akkadian Records	Ebla Archive	Old Kingdom Records	Early Bronze Age
	Irikagina Edict			
2000	Neo-Sumerian Records			
	Laws of Ur-Namma			
	Old Babylonian Records	Old Assyrian Records	Middle Kingdom Records	Middle Bronze Age
	Laws of Lipit-Ishtar	Alalakh VII Archive		
	Laws of Eshnunna	Hazor Document		
	Laws of Hammurabi			
1500	*Ammi-Ṣaduqa Edict*			
	Middle Babylonian Records	Alalakh IV Archive	*Horem-Heb Edict*	Late Bronze Age
		Emar Archive		
	Nuzi Archive	**Hittite Laws**	Deir el-Medina Archive	
	Middle Assyrian Records	Ugarit Archive		
	Middle Assyrian Laws	*Tudhalia IV Edict*		
1000				
	Neo-Assyrian Records	**Covenant Code (?)**	Hieratic Records	Iron Age
	Neo-Babylonian Records	**Deuteronomic Code**		
	Neo-Babylonian Laws	Laws of Drakon		
		Yavneh Yam Inscription	Demotic Records	
500		**Gortyn Code**		
		Priestly Code (?)	Elephantine Archive	Persian Empire
		Twelve Tables		
300				
		Dead Sea Scrolls		Hellenistic
0				
		Josephus		Roman and Persian
		Philo		
		Mishnah		
		Mekhiltah		
		Greek Translations (Septuagint)		
		Targums		
		Vulgate		
500				
		Masoretic Text (MT)		

Introduction

1. APPROACH AND METHOD

To call this book an introduction to biblical law is to do it both justice and injustice. It is certainly about the Bible, but only the canonical books of the Jewish tradition, namely, the Hebrew Bible (Old Testament). This excludes the Greek Bible (New Testament), as well as the Apocrypha and other Second Temple literature. (Henceforth, "Bible" and "biblical" refer to the Hebrew Bible, unless otherwise stated.)

This book is also certainly about biblical law, but for a number of biblical scholars that means primarily the rules of a purely religious nature, as to what foods to eat, what clothes to wear, what rituals to observe. For many who are interested in theology, these rules are the quintessence of biblical law, in that they regulate the relationship between God and humans. There is therefore no clear dividing line between laws and moral precepts.

The focus of the book is rather on law as understood by jurists. It comprises those rules that regulate relationships between humans who are the members of a society in the conduct of their everyday lives, protecting their economic, social, corporal, and psychological interests. Those rules establish rights and duties that can be enforced in a court of law. They fall into categories that are applicable in any developed legal system, such as property, inheritance, contracts, crimes, and evidence. Although outnumbered by religious rules and moral precepts, many such rules are found in the Bible.

The book is an introduction, not a scholarly monograph. It is designed as an elementary textbook for readers who do not necessarily know Hebrew but are familiar with the Hebrew Bible (or are prepared to familiarize themselves) through an English translation. For the sake of consistency and to facilitate its use as a course book, the Jewish Publication Society Tanakh (JPS) is taken as the default translation (see Further Reading at the end of this introduction).[1] Since every translation is an interpretation, however, and the interpretation of legal verses presumes an interpretation of the law itself, the authors when citing passages have given their own translation, which may differ significantly from the JPS.

While it unrepentantly represents the authors' point of view resulting from a combined five decades of studying and teaching the subject, the book also tries to summarize current scholarship in the field. Nonetheless, it does not cover a great deal of what would ordinarily be considered scholarship on biblical law. Most of that scholarship is concerned with the law in the Bible: the composition of biblical verses of legal content, their redaction, their relationship to each other in terms of which came first and which influenced the other, and how that influence is expressed in their formulation. This book is concerned rather with the texts of the Bible within the context of ancient Israelite law: the Bible as evidence for the practice and theory of law in the society that engendered it. The Bible is best known as a religious document, but it is also the record of a society—that of ancient Israel—in various political forms, whether as tribes or kingdoms or provinces, over hundreds of years during the first millennium BCE. It is by far the most important primary source of the law of that society, but it is still only an evidentiary source. Questions not only of the composition of the text but also of the chronology of the laws are for the most part irrelevant or unhelpful, for reasons that will be discussed below.

As an introductory textbook, the book contains few footnotes, which are of an explanatory nature and not scholarly references. Instead, suggestions for further reading are given at the end of each chapter, and a full bibliography is given at the end of the book, including more advanced works that assume knowledge of Hebrew and sometimes of other ancient languages, such as Akkadian and Greek. The bibliography also includes modern scholarship in French and German. For any student wishing to study biblical law in depth, these ancient and modern languages are essential tools.

2. EVERYDAY LAW

Although the category of everyday law is a modern one, ancient sources do show some awareness of its distinctiveness. The edges are not sharply delineated, however: everyday and religious law may overlap, with some laws falling

1. This means that we also follow the numbering of chapters and verses in the JPS translation. At times, therefore, our references will differ slightly from those that would apply to translations (e.g., KJV, NIV, NRSV) that follow the numbering system found in Christian traditions.

into either category or playing a transitional role. Nor should the categories be identified simply with a division between secular and sacred. The divine sphere was regarded as an integral component in an ancient legal system, with its own role to play, in areas as diverse as the law of evidence and the law of contract.

In modern legal theory, the distinction between legal rules and moral precepts is primarily a question of sanctions. Breach of a law is met with an organized response of the society, in the form of coercive sanction, ranging from refusal to enforce rights engendered by the action to pecuniary and physical penalties. Breach of a moral precept is met with disapproval by members of the society or a sanction by a suprasocietal being such as a deity. In ancient legal systems, where deities were regarded as part of the system and divine sanctions were deemed as efficacious as human sanctions, the distinction between law and morality cannot be so sharply defined. An exhortatory response unaccompanied by a sanction, a purely divine sanction, or the absence of a human sanction in the text of the law—all these are rough criteria for identifying a rule as moral rather than legal. Arguments from silence, however, are to be treated with caution: there may have been human sanctions that the text either assumed were obvious to the contemporary reader or for other reasons did not see fit to mention explicitly.

We cannot be sure of the extent to which the laws set out in the Bible were actually put into practice during the Iron Age—the time of ancient Israel and Judah. As we shall see, some of them may have been purely utopian; some were rules of practice transfigured by ideology; and others, although pragmatic in content, were most probably the product of academic circles, that is, of groups of scribes engaged in a theoretical endeavor. Nonetheless, the laws in the Bible represent in many instances what people at the time considered the law to be, and, even if not always put into practice, they reveal the underlying processes of juridical thought that were prevalent in the society.

It is worth noting that a number of scholars disagree with this particular perspective. They see no evidence to support the assertion that the laws in the Bible represent to any significant extent the everyday law of ancient Israel. It is more reasonable, they would say, to assume that the laws in the Bible were never put into practice and that any overlap that might be discovered between biblical law and the everyday law of Israel is merely coincidental. While we believe that evidence adduced later in this book supports our view, we offer three points as an initial response. First, due to a scarcity of documents from Israel dating to the biblical period, it is fair to say that we have very little evidence from the Iron Age itself of ancient Israel's everyday law. Second, it is also fair to say that we have abundant evidence regarding the everyday law of Israel's neighbors, in the form of hundreds of thousands of extant documents, especially from Mesopotamia (see below). Third, there is a fair amount of overlap—in terms of specific rules and legal reasoning—between the biblical and the peri-biblical material. Thus one is faced with explaining this overlap. Is it coincidence? Were the biblical authors seeking to replicate parts of the law they knew to exist in other societies? Or is it reasonable to suppose that these authors' texts reflect many aspects of their own society's everyday law? We opt for the latter.

3. ISRAEL AND ITS NEIGHBORS

For most of its history, the polities that made up biblical Israel enjoyed a precarious existence on the edge of great empires, into which they were occasionally absorbed. The Bible traces a development through the following political forms: patriarchal household, nation enslaved, tribal confederation, unified kingdom, divided kingdoms, province. Only the last two forms are recorded in external sources, from the ninth to the third century.

In the Late Bronze Age (late second millennium), the Near East was divided up between a number of great powers, most notably Egypt, Hatti (the domain of the Hittites), Babylonia, and Assyria. Canaan, not yet showing signs of Israelite occupation, was divided into a mosaic of petty kingdoms, most of which were vassal states of the Egyptian Empire. In Syria, the Hittites held sway, replacing the fading star of the Hurrian Empire (Mittanni), while behind them lurked the growing power of Assyria and its archrival, Babylonia. The patriarchal narratives depict a setting at the beginning of this period (or even a little earlier) and the exodus and presettlement narratives a setting toward the end.

This world of great powers was brought to an end toward the close of the millennium, due in part to large population movements. The Hittite kingdom and its empire were destroyed, Egypt lost its empire in Asia, and Assyria and Babylonia were severely weakened. For a while, a power vacuum allowed small groups in the central highlands of Palestine—groups from which the state of ancient Israel likely emerged—to maintain an independent existence. It is portrayed in the Bible as a period of tribal confederation, followed by the united monarchy under Saul, David, and Solomon.

By the eighth century Assyria had recovered and was on a path to expansion. Over the next hundred years, it emerged as the supreme power of the region, conquering Mesopotamia, Syria-Palestine, and for a brief period even Egypt. In the seventh century, the kingdoms of Israel and Judah, both Assyrian vassals, joined local coalitions in revolt against Assyrian hegemony. Israel was destroyed and its population exiled, while Judah just managed to survive as a vassal.

In 612 BCE a coalition of Babylonia and the Medes defeated the Assyrian Empire. For Judah, the Babylonian overlord replaced the Assyrian until 586, when an unsuccessful revolt resulted in Judah's dissolution, the destruction of its temple in Jerusalem, and the exile of its elite to Babylonia. In 539, Babylonia in turn fell to the Persians, who established an empire stretching across the whole of the Near East. Judah was reconstituted as a province of the Persian Empire, and returning exiles, under the leadership of Ezra the scribe and subsequently of Nehemiah, were allowed to rebuild the Jerusalem temple. In 332, Alexander the Great destroyed the Persian Empire and ushered in Hellenistic rule, which marks the end of the events recorded by the Hebrew Bible.[2]

Further Reading

Some titles have been abbreviated; see bibliography for full citations.

Buss, M. J. 1989. "Logic and Israelite Law," 49–65.
Patrick, D. 1989. "Studying Biblical Law as a Humanities," 27–47.
Wells, B. 2008. "What Is Biblical Law?" 223–43.
Wenham, G. J. 1997. "The Gap between Law and Ethics in the Bible," 17–29.

General Reference Works That Should Be Consulted Throughout

Civilizations of the Ancient Near East. Edited by J. M. Sasson. 4 vols. New York: Scribner, 1995. Encyclopedia articles on political, social, and cultural history, arranged by theme and civilization.

Anchor Bible Dictionary. Edited by D. N. Freedman. 6 vols. New York: Doubleday, 1992. Encyclopedia articles arranged alphabetically.

A History of Ancient Near Eastern Law. Edited by R. Westbrook. Leiden: Brill, 2003. Chapters in geographical and chronological order; uniform legal topics within each chapter.

Anchor Bible. Edited by D. N. Freedman. New York: Doubleday, 1964. Series of individual translations and commentaries of biblical books; series not yet complete.

International Critical Commentary. New York: Doubleday, 1899. Old but classic series of commentaries, especially useful for books missing from the Anchor Bible series.

Tanakh: The Holy Scriptures. Philadelphia: Jewish Publication Society, 1985. Translation of the Hebrew Bible.

Falk, Z. W. *Hebrew Law in Biblical Times*. 2nd ed. Provo, UT: Brigham Young University Press, 2001. Introduction to the law of the Hebrew Bible through the perspective of a scholar of rabbinic law.

Patrick, D. *Old Testament Law*. Atlanta: John Knox Press, 1985. Introduction to the law of the Hebrew Bible through the perspective of a scholar of biblical religion.

2. The book of Daniel, although it purports to be set in the period of the Persian Empire, most likely comes from the mid-160s BCE and chronicles in symbolic language much of the reign of Antiochus IV, a Greek ruler of the Seleucid territories who ruled from 175 to 164. Thus the text of Daniel and perhaps parts of other biblical books as well (e.g., Esther, Ecclesiastes) likely come from the Hellenistic period.

Questions for Review

1. When this book uses the terms “Bible” and “biblical,” to what is it referring?
   a. The Christian Bible, consisting of both the Old Testament and the New Testament
   b. The Hebrew Bible or Tanakh
   c. The Catholic Old Testament
   d. The Protestant Old Testament
2. Which of the following statements best defines “everyday law” as this book uses the expression?
   a. Everyday law refers to the religious and moral precepts that people were expected to follow in their everyday lives.
   b. Everyday law is essentially synonymous with the term “biblical law,” since the laws in the Bible are the laws that were practiced in ancient Israel.
   c. Everyday law refers to the laws that were practiced in ancient Israel’s legal system.
3. What is one way of explaining the fact that a number of biblical laws contain rules that are actually put into practice in ancient Near Eastern societies other than Israel?
4. When is it likely that the state of ancient Israel began to emerge?
   a. during the power vacuum in Palestine that followed the end of the Late Bronze Age
   b. shortly after the year 2000 BCE when Abraham, Isaac, and Jacob lived
   c. in the middle of the Late Bronze Age with the mass escape of the Israelites from Egypt
5. Put the following ancient Near Eastern empires in chronological order.
   a. Neo-Babylonian
   b. Neo-Assyrian
   c. Greek
   d. Persian

Answers

1. It is reasonable to say that both (b) and (d) are correct. The contents of the Hebrew Bible (b) and the Protestant Old Testament (d) are exactly the same. But the order of the books and the numbering of the verses is somewhat different in both collections. Because this book follows the traditional Jewish ordering and versification of the books, the correct answer is technically (b). The Catholic Old Testament contains what is in the Hebrew Bible but includes the so-called Apocrypha or Deuterocanonical Books.
2. The correct answer is (c). There is a distinction, albeit unclear at times in the ancient world, between legal rules and moral precepts. In addition, there is only a partial overlap between the laws in the Bible and the laws that were likely practiced in ancient Israel.

3. See the chapter's section on "Everyday Law," especially the last two paragraphs.
4. The correct answer is (a). The degree to which the so-called patriarchal period and the alleged period of the exodus reflect historical reality is unknown. The first archaeological evidence of anything that might be considered representative of ancient Israel comes from the early Iron Age.
5. Neo-Assyrian, Neo-Babylonian, Persian, Greek. The chapter did not use the "Neo" prefix, but it is often used to distinguish these particular empires from older ones.

1

Sources

In this chapter, readers will discover the ancient sources that scholars use in their efforts to reconstruct ancient Israel's legal system. These include sources from ancient Israel, as well as sources from other ancient Near Eastern societies. The chapter will also explain why these sources cannot always be taken at face value and why scholars often disagree on how to read and interpret them.

1. HEBREW BIBLE

The Hebrew term for the Bible is "Tanakh," an acronym derived from the names of its three main components: Torah, Nevi'im, and Ketuvim. *Torah*, meaning "law," is the name given to the first five books of the Bible, also known in English as the Pentateuch. After the creation and the early history of humanity, they contain an account of Israelite history from the patriarchs to the moment of entry into the promised land, as well as a large number of laws that are said to have been dictated by God to Moses, either at Mount Sinai or at various stages of the Israelites' journey through the desert.

Nevi'im means "prophets" and consists of the continuing history of Israel from Joshua to Kings, plus the works of the canonical prophets (Isaiah, Jeremiah, etc.). *Ketuvim* ("writings") are all the remaining books. The canon and present order of the books was settled by Rabbis of the Greco-Roman period. (In the Christian Old Testament, the order is somewhat different.) Division into chapters and verses, as found in modern editions, was achieved only in the Middle Ages.

The Hebrew text that is now used as the standard version is the Masoretic Text (MT), edited by the Masoretes, a group of scholars active in Tiberias from approximately the seventh through the tenth century CE. The oldest complete manuscript, the Leningrad Codex (early eleventh century CE), derives from this tradition. The accuracy of the Masoretes' editing was demonstrated with the discovery of the Dead Sea Scrolls, which contained manuscripts of parts of the Bible dating between the third and first centuries BCE.

Hebrew writing was originally purely consonantal. The present system of vowels (called "pointing") that are added in a standard Hebrew Bible was also invented by the Masoretes. Because of the grammatical structure of the language, it is in fact unnecessary to write in the vowels, which can be supplied automatically by a native speaker (and readers of modern Hebrew newspapers and novels). The consonantal text can be ambiguous, however, and the Masoretes were concerned to establish an authoritative text for the Holy Scripture, whose language had long ceased to be a spoken language. (Its pronunciation had been preserved through the tradition of reading aloud in synagogues.) Their pointing, however, reflects their own interpretation. It is possible to change the meaning by simply changing the vowels, while leaving the consonantal text intact, and many modern scholars do so.

The Bible represents a compendium of the national literature of Israel over a period of nearly a thousand years. During that time, it underwent a process of editing and adaptation, which makes the dating of its component parts, except for obvious chronological points of reference to a *terminus post quem*, highly speculative. The earliest passages may go back as far as the twelfth century BCE, while the last words were probably written in the second century BCE. Most of the books appear to have been composed or taken their final form between the seventh and fourth centuries.

The dating of individual books and of passages within books is one of the main issues of biblical studies, and one that scholars continue to debate obsessively. A complicating factor is the documentary hypothesis. When scholars of the Enlightenment first began to read the biblical texts critically, it was noticed that passages within the books of Torah appear to have been written by different hands, since they differ in language (especially the names used for God), style, and ideology. Moreover, repetitions and inconsistencies that traditional interpreters had tried to reconcile could be explained by the existence of separate sources within the text.

The theory, as developed during the nineteenth century, is that there are at least four distinct sources within the Torah: J (the Yahwist), E (the Elohist), P (the Priestly source) and D (the Deuteronomic source). This last recognizes the separate authorship of the book of Deuteronomy, but the first three sources are said to be interwoven in the remaining books of the Pentateuch by the work of a redactor or redactors. The dating of the different sources has been the focus of the most intense debate in biblical scholarship. When applied to the legal content that makes up much of the Torah, this approach, known as the source-critical approach, has focused scholarly attention primarily on the question of which laws preceded which.

A complementary theory developed during the twentieth century is known as the form-critical approach. As applied to legal texts, the theory is based on two assumptions. First, law evolves by a process that reflects the evolution of human society from primitive to more sophisticated structures. Second, the form of a law will differ according to the sociological context of its creation (its *Sitz im Leben*). Thus the individual laws of the Torah can be read like a fossil record, their form showing telltale traces not only of their original formulation but of subtle changes made to the drafting due to evolutionary developments. In this way, inconsistencies not only between laws but even within the same law can be explained diachronically.

The source-critical and form-critical approaches have cast a long shadow over the study of biblical law. They are certainly of vital importance to anyone interested in the literary question of how the biblical text was written. For our purposes, however, the Bible is not the goal of our inquiry but a mere tool, one source of evidence among others. Fortunately, for reasons that will soon become apparent, diachronic theories have only limited relevance to the reconstruction of ancient Israelite law.

Historical evidence for the law can come from a wide variety of sources, not necessarily legal. Stories, sayings, prayers, and poems can all provide valuable insights into legal concepts and practice. While a "commandment" provides us with a direct statement of a legal norm, it may be a tendentious reshaping of the existing law for ideological purposes. The passing mention of a law in a narrative may give only indirect evidence of its existence but may be more reliable, because it occurred unself-consciously, without concern for the law's implications. We will examine a variety of different sources within the Bible.

A. Law Codes

The most famous code associated with the Bible is the Ten Commandments, but the Torah (Pentateuch) contains many more commandments—613 in all, according to rabbinic tradition. Of these, about 60 are what we would call provisions of everyday law. They are unevenly spread through the second to fifth books of the Torah. Nearly half are to be found in chapters 21 and 22 of Exodus, in a context that has often been associated with the Elohist (E) source.[1] An equal number are found in the book of Deuteronomy, mostly concentrated in chapters 21 and 22, but with scattered examples from chapter 15 to chapter 25. A smaller group of laws is found in Leviticus 18–20, and a few isolated examples elsewhere in Leviticus and Numbers. The latter two books are largely attributed to the Priestly (P) source.

The bulk of the laws in the Torah are thus concentrated in three main clusters. The first, in Exodus 21 and 22:1–16, is usually called the Mishpatim (after the Hebrew term that introduces this section and means "verdicts" or "decisions"). It forms a solid block of laws covering the topics slavery, homicide, injury, damage to property and loss of property. It is preceded by the Ten Commandments and followed, after some transitional provisions (Exod. 22:17–19), by a series of ethical rules, moral exhortations, and cultic regulations. The transitional provisions deal with capital crimes that are considered a danger to the whole community: witchcraft, bestiality, and apostasy. The larger unit containing the Mishpatim is referred to as the Covenant Code (Exod. 20:22–23:33).

The second cluster, in chapters 15 to 25 of Deuteronomy, has a central block in chapters 21 and 22 that is divided by a group of ethical rules (Deut. 22:1–12). Other provisions are scattered through the remaining chapters among mostly ethical and exhortatory material. Unlike the Mishpatim, which are for the most part untouched by the style of their literary frame, the characteristic moral rhetoric of Deuteronomy attaches itself even to everyday laws: for example, legal sanctions are adorned with admonishments such as "you will purge the evil from among you, and all Israel will hear and be afraid" (Deut. 21:21). The topics covered in the Deuteronomic laws are more varied: slavery and debt-release, homicide, injury, property and inheritance, sexual offenses, family law, evidence, and punishment. Four of its laws overlap with those of the Mishpatim: slavery (Exod. 21:1–11 and Deut. 15:12–18), homicide (Exod. 21:12–14 and Deut. 19:1–13), kidnapping (Exod. 21:6 and Deut. 24:7), and seduction (Exod. 22:15–16 and Deut. 22:28–29).

The third cluster, in Leviticus 18–20, is almost exclusively concerned with sexual offenses, which are relevant to priestly concerns with purity. Other laws in the Priestly source reflect the priestly role in the taking of evidence (Lev. 5:1; 5:20–26; Num. 5:5–31), but there are two notable topics dealt with at length: homicide (Num. 35:9–34) and property (Lev. 25).

There are actually three different versions of the Ten Commandments. Many scholars have associated the one found in Exodus 34:11–26 (see Exod. 34:28 for the phrase "ten commandments") with the Yahwist (J) source. It

1. Readers should note, however, that the mere existence of an Elohist source has been called into serious question by recent scholarship. Alternative source-critical theories are appearing now on a regular basis in the scholarly literature. A new consensus has not yet been reached.

includes only cultic stipulations and is the version least familiar to modern readers. It also differs considerably from the other two versions, those from the Priestly (P) source and the Deuteronomic (D) source. These are found in Exodus 20:1–17 and Deuteronomy 5:6–21 and contain only slight differences between them. They stand apart from the other clusters of laws and were clearly intended to form a separate unit. They are not, however, laws in any meaningful sense. They contain no sanctions, and there is no hint that they ever played a role in the Israelite courts. They merely state commands or prohibitions, some of which are identifiable with social conduct (prohibition on stealing) but others only with a state of mind (prohibition on coveting). Those commandments that are identifiable with social conduct are in fact duplicated by laws elsewhere in the Torah.

Scholars have not been able to resist the temptation to attribute to the Ten Commandments a role in the Israelite legal system. Phillips (1970) claims that they were Israel's early criminal code—a closed list of the offenses that carried the death penalty. Kaufman (1978) argues that they were the organizing principle for the other laws set out, apparently at random, in Deuteronomy. As is often the case in the study of biblical law, the analysis applies to a few instances, even strikingly so, but attempts to make it a comprehensive principle inevitably lead to strained and fanciful interpretations, when the rest of the evidence will not quite fit. So while the Ten Commandments contain useful information about the law, they should not be viewed as a source on a par with a collection such as the Mishpatim.

B. Precedents

There are four cases recorded by the Priestly source where a doubtful case is brought before Moses. Moses consults God and receives a decision, which is then expressed as a binding precedent for the future, sometimes even being formulated as a general rule. The cases are the Israelite who pronounced God's name in blasphemy (Lev. 24:10–23), a second passover sacrifice for persons who happened to be unclean at the time of the first (Num. 9:1–14), a person who gathered sticks on the Sabbath (Num. 15:32–36), and the inheritance rights of the daughters of Zelophehad (Num. 27:1–11; 36). A further example from the book of Samuel is the decision of David as military commander to divide the booty between the combat and the reserve troops, which became "a fixed rule for Israel, continuing to the present day" (1 Sam. 30:22–26).

Whether these cases record historical reality is unimportant. By attributing a current rule to a particular type of legal process, they reveal a consciousness of judicial precedent as a valid source of law, which must derive from the workings of the legal system in practice. Like the law codes, they are direct evidence—and may be tendentious as to the law—but their purpose was more likely to explain how the law came to be what it is, rather than to propound what it should be.

C. Juridical Parables

The narratives of Samuel and Kings contain three stories about violation of the law that are told to a king who has committed an analogous offense, in order that the king will be led unwittingly to pass judgment on himself. They are the parable of the poor man's lamb (2 Sam. 12:1–14), the woman of Tekoah (2 Sam. 14:1–20), and the negligent guard (1 Kgs. 20:35–43). In each case, the story has to be legally realistic and to engage accepted legal principles, in order to deceive the king into exercising his judicial powers.

A slightly different type of parable is found in the prophetic books. In the parables of the vineyard (Isa. 5:1–7) and of the faithless wife (Jer. 3:1–5), an everyday situation is used as a metaphor for the relationship between God and Israel. Legal consequences of the situation are used as part of the metaphor. Again, realism of both facts and law is necessary for the credibility of the analogy.

Similar uses of metaphor are found in other prophetic allegories (e.g., Ezek. 16:1–42; 23:1–10; Hos. 2:1–20). The consequences of the wrongdoing of Israel, portrayed as an unfaithful wife, provide telling evidence of the law of marriage and divorce in practice. The law is not, however, as directly engaged here in the polemic, and the situations described are not as consistent in their attachment to realism or to the metaphor.

D. Legal Narratives

There are many stories in the Bible recounting a legal action or transaction, or an illegal act and its consequences, which provide indirect evidence of the practice of law. For example, the story of Judah and Tamar in Genesis 38 provides an application of the levirate that is not discussed in the levirate law in Deuteronomy 25:5–10. The narrative does not set out the rules; it assumes that the reader is familiar with the law and mentions only as many details as are necessary for the story. The sale of land is not included in any of the law codes, but two narratives recount the steps of a sale, each emphasizing that the legal requirements were punctiliously followed, so that the validity of the sale might not be called into question (Gen. 23; Jer. 32:1–15).

2. ISRAELITE

The text of the Bible has been transmitted to us by copying and recopying, the oldest extant witnesses (among the Dead Sea Scrolls, dated between the third and the first century BCE) still being hundreds of years later than the date of the original composition of most of the biblical books. Thus it is not surprising that the dating of the laws transmitted with it is uncertain. Documents discovered in archaeological excavations in the land of Israel that date from the biblical period would provide a much more reliable witness. Only a handful of such documents has been recovered thus far. A few cuneiform legal texts from the Neo-Assyrian period have survived (Horowitz et al. 2006).[2] They appear to relate to transactions such as sales and loans, and a couple of texts contain Hebrew names. But these records are short, fragmentary, and not very conducive to legal analysis. The most helpful document to date is the Yavneh Yam inscription. Discovered at a site near Ashqelon, it dates to the seventh century and is a petition by a workman to the local governor regarding his garment. The amount of law to be gleaned from it, though, is still very small and is further reduced by difficulties of translation. Unfortunately, a few other records supposedly from the same period, in particular the Moussaieff Ostraca, have had their authenticity questioned (Eph'al and Naveh 1998; Rollston 2003).

3. POSTBIBLICAL

A. Commentaries

The study and interpretation of the laws of the Torah began already in the biblical period with Ezra the scribe. It was continued by the Rabbis, the earliest school of which was known as the Tannaim. Among the early rabbinic commentaries on the Torah, the Mekhilta de-Rabbi Ishmael is the most important. It represents a Tannaitic exposition of the book of Exodus, with a juridical commentary on the laws contained in that book. Another early rabbinic commentary called the Sifra contains an exposition of the laws of Leviticus.

The other major commentary of this period is that of Philo of Alexandria, a Jewish philosopher of the first century CE. He wrote a discourse in Greek on the Laws of Moses, as well as books on the Ten Commandments and on the Special Laws, that is, all the other laws of the Torah.

B. The "Oral Law"

According to rabbinic teaching, Moses received on Mount Sinai not only the written Torah but also the oral law, a vast compendium of oral traditions.

2. In addition, one Persian-period cuneiform tablet from the site of Mikhmoret (identified in Horowitz et al. 2006 as Mikhmoret 1) is said to contain a slave-sale contract and is to be published in the near future (Horowitz et al. 2006: 109).

They were written down first in the Mishnah, a compilation dating to the second century CE and in much larger format in the Talmud, compiled in the fifth century CE. These collections are essentially the jurisprudence of the Rabbis (Tannaim and later Amora'im) starting in the Hellenistic period.

In the first century CE, Josephus, a general in the Jewish revolt who was captured by the Romans and became a Roman citizen, produced a history of the Jews (*Jewish Antiquities*) that contains paraphrases of biblical laws. It includes rules not found in the biblical text, some of which may derive from rabbinic traditions.

The importance of the postbiblical translations, commentaries, and compendia is that until recently they were the only source for our interpretation of biblical law. The meaning of the laws of the Torah and even of individual Hebrew words in the laws was mediated through them. Consciously or unconsciously, all modern translations and scholarship go back to the Hellenistic sources.

It is true that earlier traditions are preserved in the later sources. Some may go back as far as the biblical period, but which ones is a moot question. At the same time, the early Rabbis were not historians, intent solely on preserving or restoring the most authentic ancient version. Like lawyers of any period, their purpose was to produce from their inherited source, the Torah, a body of law that made sense in terms of their own society. That society was the Hellenistic world, which embodied a mode of thought utterly different from that of the biblical world.

C. Greek Bible (New Testament)

Much of what has been said about the Rabbis applies to the Greek Bible. It is the product of Hellenistic thought and looks upon the Hebrew Bible as an old text to be translated and interpreted. It therefore contains important interpretations of biblical laws, but as with the Rabbis, their purpose was to adapt the older text to present circumstances, not to provide a history lesson. The Greek Bible also contains some allusions to oral-law traditions that may go back to the biblical period.

D. Translations

The tradition that ensured the recopying of the biblical text also gave rise to interpretation of its contents. The Septuagint represents translations of the Hebrew Bible into Greek, with fragmentary witnesses dating from as early as the second century, although the earliest major manuscript is from the fourth century CE. As every translation is an interpretation, the Septuagint gives us an idea of how the biblical laws were understood in the Hellenistic period. The same applies to early Aramaic translations of the Bible called the Targums, which represent rabbinic interpretation. The Vulgate is a translation into Latin, from the Hebrew and the Greek, mostly by Jerome in the fourth century CE.

Modern translations often derive as much from these early translations as from the Hebrew text. The ancient interpretations they preserve have shaped all traditional English translations. Only in the late twentieth century has the growing knowledge of rediscovered ancient languages like Akkadian and Ugaritic come to influence scholarly interpretation, leading sometimes to radically new translations.

Nowhere are the tensions between different interpretations more acute than in the translation of biblical laws. Ancient translations do not always agree on the meaning of key Hebrew terms, and even when the terminology is not in question, the legal meaning of a law, as that law is rendered in an ancient translation, may be influenced chiefly by the contemporary, ahistorical concerns of Hellenistic exegetes or rabbinic jurists. These discrepancies are then magnified in later, traditional translations and may even be compounded by modern translations, since the existence of newly discovered parallels from ancient sources is not necessarily a key to unlocking the secrets of the Hebrew text. On the contrary, the ancient legal sources themselves may be difficult to interpret.

A good illustration of the problems of translating biblical laws is the law regarding injury to a pregnant woman in the Mishpatim (Exod. 21:22–25). The ruling is rendered obscure in part by apparent nonsequiturs in the text, but above all by the appearance of two rare terms (*'asown* and *be-flylym*), the legal meaning of which emerges neither from their immediate context nor from their few occurrences elsewhere in the Bible. The *Authorized Version* (King James Bible, from the seventeenth century) renders the passage this way:

> If men strive, and hurt a woman with child, so that her fruit depart from her, and yet no mischief (*'asown*) follows: he shall be surely punished, according as the woman's husband will lay upon him, and he shall pay as the judges determine (*be-flylym*). And if any mischief follow, then thou shalt give life for life, eye for eye, tooth for tooth, hand for hand, foot for foot, burning for burning, wound for wound, stripe for stripe.

The AV does not explain what "mischief" implies, and the recent *Jewish Publication Society* translation is equally vague:

> When men fight, and one of them pushes a pregnant woman and a miscarriage results, but no other damage ensues, the one responsible shall be fined according as the woman's husband may exact from him, the payment to be based on reckoning. But if other damage ensues, the penalty shall be life for life, eye for eye. . . .

Their reticence is due to an embarrassing disagreement among the ancient translations on which they depend for their interpretation. The *Septuagint* renders the verse,

> If two men fight and they strike a pregnant woman, and her child comes out not fully formed (*'asown = exeikonismenon*), he shall surely be punished; as much as the husband of the woman shall impose on him, he shall give with an appropriate [payment?] (*be-flylym = meta axiomatos*). If it is fully formed, he shall give life for life, eye for eye. . . .

By contrast, *Targum Onkelos* translates:

> If men fight and they strike a pregnant woman and her child comes out and it is not death, he shall have exacted as much as the husband of the woman shall impose on him and he shall give according to the word of the judges. And if it is death, you shall give life for life. . . .

The *Vulgate* follows the Targum rather than the Septuagint, but is more explicit:

> If men brawl and someone strikes a pregnant woman and causes a miscarriage but she herself lives (*ipsa vixerit*), he shall be liable to damages as much as the husband of the woman demands and the judges shall judge. But if her death follows, he shall give back life for life, eye for eye. . . .

The Septuagint also translates the term *be-flylym* differently from the Targum and the Vulgate, but even the latter vary in their treatment of the role of the "judges," being uncertain as to how they come into the picture when the victim's husband is responsible for determining the level of damages. The two modern translations cited above present totally different interpretations on this point.

Finally, it should be noted that all of these translations vary in their faithfulness to the grammar of the original. Some make changes in order to make the translation conform to what they deem to be a more comprehensible law. Thus the Hebrew "they strike a pregnant woman" (third-person masculine plural) is sometimes rendered in the singular and the verb in the phrase "you shall give life for life" (second-person masculine singular) is sometimes rendered with the third person. Modern scholars, albeit relying on ancient Near Eastern parallels, have not reached agreement on the legal issues raised by these discrepancies; if anything, their interpretations are further apart, as we shall see below (chapter 4: Crimes and Delicts).

Another law, a provision concerning intercourse with a female slave in Leviticus 19:20–22, illustrates a special problem facing translators of the Hebrew text, namely, the *hapax legomenon*, a Greek term for a word that occurs only once in the Bible. Lacking other contexts, modern interpretation must rely on the analogy of words based on a similar root, which may have nothing to do with the word in question, or on the ancient translations, which themselves often show signs of guesswork in such cases.

Leviticus 19:20 is remarkable in containing not one but two *hapax* words:

> If a man lies with a woman sexually and she is a slave *nehrefet* to a man and has not been redeemed and freedom has not been granted her, there shall be *biqqoret*; they shall not be put to death because she was not freed.

The *Septuagint* translates:

> And if someone sleeps with a woman sexually and she is a slave kept (*diapephylagmenē*) for a man and has not been redeemed and freedom has not been granted her, there shall be an inspection (*episkopē*); they shall not die because she was not freed.

The *Vulgate* differs:

> A man if he sleeps sexually with a woman who is a slave and also marriageable (*nubilis*) but has not been redeemed nor given in freedom, they shall beat (*vapulabunt*) them both; they shall not die because she was not free.

The *Authorized Version* follows the Septuagint for the first *hapax* and the Vulgate for the second:

> And whosoever lieth carnally with a woman, that is a bondmaid, betrothed to an husband, and not at all redeemed, nor freedom given her, she shall be scourged; they shall not be put to death, because she was not free.

The *New Revised Standard Version* follows the Septuagint throughout:

> If a man has sexual relations with a woman who is a slave, designated for another man but not ransomed or given her freedom, an inquiry shall be held. They shall not be put to death, since she has not been freed.

The *JPS* relies on new scholarship to offer a different approach:

> If a man has carnal relations with a woman who is a slave and has been designated for another man, but has not been redeemed or given her freedom, there shall be an indemnity; they shall not, however, be put to death, since she has not been freed.

JPS translates *biqqoret* as indemnity, relying on an Akkadian cognate: *baqru* "(legal) claim." Westbrook (1990) uses further instruments available to the modern scholar, arguing that *baqru* means specifically a claim for return of property, associating *nehrefet* with a root meaning "to pledge," and also changing the pointing of the words "woman" and "man":

> If a man has sexual relations with a wife, she being pledged to the man, there shall be a claim for return (of the wife). They shall not be put to death. . . .

None of these translations, ancient or modern, can simply be taken as the definitive interpretation. Consequently, it is wise even for a reader who does not know Hebrew to use annotated translations that alert the reader to the existence of a *hapax*, or better still, a scholarly biblical commentary that discusses textual problems.

Finally, even the consonantal Hebrew text on which translators rely can be ambiguous. There may, of course, be discrepancies between manuscripts. Even within the standard Masoretic Text, however, the Masoretes noted a discrepancy between how a word was traditionally written (*ketiv*) and how it was traditionally read (*qere'*). This can affect the meaning of a law, as in Exodus 21:8, where the situation of a female slave will differ according to whether she is in the hands of an owner "who did not assign her" (*ketiv*) or "who assigned her to himself" (*qere'*). Translations must choose between the two traditions in each instance but do not always indicate that an alternative reading exists.

4. PERI-BIBLICAL

A. Ancient Near East

Meaningful historical study of biblical law is only possible thanks to the explosion of discoveries in the ancient Near East over the past hundred years. Whole civilizations that were lost have been recovered from the periods contemporary with and prior to biblical Israel. Legal documents in the tens of thousands have been recovered, setting the biblical records in context and placing them in an entirely different light.

Records from Egypt

Legal documents in Egypt were written mostly on perishable materials that have not survived. For this reason, it is difficult to judge the Egyptian influence on biblical law. An archive of several hundred ostraca written in hieratic script from Deir el-Medina in the Late Bronze Age (thirteenth and twelfth centuries) is the largest source for the earlier periods. Documentation becomes abundant only in the Hellenistic and Roman periods with the survival in dry desert locations of archives of papyri written in demotic script.

A small archive of a few dozen papyri from Elephantine in the fifth century has an importance far beyond its size. For it contains the records in Aramaic of a Jewish community that formed part of the garrison in this outpost of the Persian Empire. It is thus a unique record of a Jewish community, albeit outside of Israel, in the biblical period.

Cuneiform Records

The largest source of supply is in cuneiform writing on clay tablets. The reason is partly the chance circumstance of preservation and partly the pattern of ancient cultural diffusion. While most materials on which records were kept, such as wood, papyrus, or parchment, are perishable, clay tablets, once baked or sun-dried, are virtually indestructible. The bulk of the tablets come from Mesopotamia, but an increasing number of discoveries is being made in Syria and Anatolia.

Cuneiform writing was invented in the late fourth millennium by a people living at the head of the Persian Gulf, whom we call the Sumerians. It was adopted by other peoples in Mesopotamia who spoke a Semitic language called Akkadian, better known in its two main dialects, Babylonian and Assyrian. The Sumerian language died out at the end of the third millennium, but Sumerian culture and learning were preserved along with their script by the Akkadian-speaking inhabitants of Mesopotamia for another two thousand years. In the second millennium, Akkadian became the lingua franca of international relations and was also widely used in Syria-Palestine and Anatolia as the language of law and administration. In the first millennium it was replaced by languages written in alphabetic scripts, but the influence of Mesopotamian culture was maintained further west by the conquests of the Assyrian and Babylonian empires.

The cuneiform legal record stretches from the twenty-sixth century to the second century. The largest number of tablets comes from Babylonia in two periods: the Old Babylonian period (ca. twentieth to sixteenth centuries, in archeological terms, the Middle Bronze Age) and the Neo-Babylonian/Persian period (ca. seventh to fourth centuries), where they number in the tens of thousands. Several thousand documents in Akkadian are furnished by fifteenth-century archives from Nuzi, a Hurrian-speaking province of the Mittannian Empire situated on the Tigris.

In Anatolia, significant archives have been found at Kanesh, an Assyrian merchants' colony in Anatolia that flourished in the eighteenth century. In the Late Bronze Age (fifteenth to eleventh centuries), Hattushah, the Hittite capital, furnishes some documents, written mostly in Hittite.

It is also from the Late Bronze Age that cuneiform archives have been found in Syria. The most important are from Emar, on the Euphrates; Alalakh, on the Orontes (where a small archive from the Middle Bronze Age was also found); and Ugarit, a seaport on the Syrian coast. Although the legal documents are in Akkadian, the inhabitants of those cities all spoke northwest Semitic languages, that is, languages more closely related to Hebrew. Indeed, at Ugarit a cuneiform alphabetic script was developed to record their own language, and while most of the writings in Ugaritic are literary in nature, there are just a few legal documents. Finally, a few cuneiform legal documents have to date been found in the territory of Israel itself. The most well-preserved is a record of a lawsuit, written in good Akkadian, and dating to the Middle Bronze.

Typology

The legal sources of the ancient Near East may be divided into two main categories. The vast bulk of the texts is records of legal transactions, such as sale, loan, lease, marriage, and adoption, to which may be added a much smaller number of records of litigation. These attest to the law in practice and are contemporary with the transactions that they record. They are, however, only indirect evidence of the law, which stands as a shadowy presence behind the transactions described. Even the litigation records do not discuss the law but confine themselves to the evidence and the verdict.

The second category consists of direct statements of the law. It is made up of a very small number of royal decrees—the nearest equivalent to modern legislation—and the so-called "law codes." The decrees focus on narrow issues of immediate impact, especially the general cancellation of debts. The law codes are much wider in scope, touching upon most major areas of law. Seven cuneiform law codes have been recovered to date (for an introduction to and full translations of these codes, see Roth 1997):

1. The Laws of Ur-Namma (LU), from the city of Ur in southern Mesopotamia; written in Sumerian and dating to around 2100
2. The Laws of Lipit-Ishtar (LL), from the city of Isin in southern Mesopotamia; written in Sumerian and dating to around 1900
3. The Laws of Eshnunna (LE), from a city of that name in northern Mesopotamia; written in Akkadian and dating to around 1800

4. The Laws of Hammurabi (LH), from the city of Babylon; written in Akkadian and dating to around 1750
5. The Middle Assyrian Laws (MAL), from the city of Assur; written in Akkadian and dating to the fourteenth century
6. The Neo-Babylonian Laws (NBL), from the city of Sippar in central Mesopotamia; written in Akkadian and dating to the seventh century
7. The Hittite Laws (HL), from Anatolia; written in cuneiform script in Hittite and dating between the sixteenth and the twelfth centuries

Each code has been assigned paragraph numbers (or, at times, paragraph letters) by modern scholarship. Thus, one will see a given paragraph referred to by the abbreviation for its code and by its paragraph number or letter (e.g., LU 2, LL b, LE 53, HL 197). In addition, the fifteen different tablets and tablet fragments that comprise MAL have been given letter designations A through O. References to paragraphs in MAL include these designations as well (e.g., MAL A 15, MAL B 2).

Affinities

This huge mass of legal sources, cuneiform and other, extending over almost three thousand years, encompasses dozens of different societies and political units, from villages to empires, and many different languages and cultures. The law that these sources represent is remarkable for two salient characteristics: continuity and conservatism. While individual rules differed from legal system to legal system—indeed, imperial powers tended to respect the legal autonomy of their vassal states—the same underlying principles continued unchanged for millennia and occur all over the region. For example, the dual legal role of the solemn oath by one's god (or gods), as a means of creating contractual promises and of affirming testimony in court, is universal, irrespective of the different religions and cults or of religious reforms. The same applies to the basic system of male inheritance: joint inheritance, followed by equal division at the initiative of the heirs, with an extra portion for the eldest son.

Affinities are occasionally found at a more specific level. A contractual penalty that involves breaking teeth is attested in third-millennium Sumer; it then disappears from the record for hundreds of years, only to reappear at Nuzi in the fifteenth century. The technical legal phrase "his heart is satisfied" has been traced in documents from Sumer to fifth-century Egypt.

All this evidence points, at the very least, to a common legal tradition that was prevalent throughout the ancient Near East. It is already in place when written records first appear in the Early Bronze Age and continues unabated into the Hellenistic period. Biblical Israel does not escape the influence of this tradition: to use the examples already given, its use of the oath and its inheritance system do not differ from the general pattern.

The affinities become even closer when we look at the special case of the law codes. All of the law codes are strikingly similar in form. Their salient characteristic is the *casuistic* sentence, namely, a conditional clause stating the circumstances of a hypothetical case, followed by a clause stating the legal consequences. For example: "If a man knocks out the eye of a man, his eye shall be knocked out" (LH 196). (In biblical scholarship, the conditional clause is referred to as the *protasis* and the consequences clause as the *apodosis*.)

The content of all of the codes is everyday law as would be practiced in the courts. The similarity in content, however, runs even deeper. Many of the same cases keep recurring in different codes, not always with identical facts or with the same solution, but close enough to show that they drew upon the same situations and the same legal principles. Again, the same cases recur in codes hundreds of years apart.

The biblical laws fit into this pattern. They are for the most part casuistic in form and contain many cases found in other law codes. In the Mishpatim we find many examples, such as the case of a man who suffers nonpermanent injury in a fight and is entitled to damages for his loss of work and medical costs (Exod. 21:18–19), which is also found in LH 206 and HL 10. From the Deuteronomic laws, the rape of a maiden who is betrothed but not married (Deut. 22:23–27) is also found in LE 26 and LH 130, while the woman who seizes a man's genitals in a fight (Deut. 25:11–12) is dealt with in MAL A 8. Indeed, the parallels between the biblical and cuneiform laws are the closest that any literary genre in the Bible has with an external source. They demonstrate that the clusters of everyday law that we have identified in the Torah are not a modern construction, but must already have had some independent existence in antiquity.

Differing models have been constructed to explain the relationship between the biblical and the cuneiform codes. The *evolutionary model* emphasizes the independent development of laws in early Israel. It was only the casuistic form and some of the content that was imported from the local societies that Israel encountered in Canaan. The difficulty with this approach is that the strong affinities of form and content with the cuneiform codes are an embarrassment that needs to be explained away. The *literary model* therefore posits a much closer dependence, in which texts like the Laws of Hammurabi were copied and imitated by Hebrew scribes. The difficulty with this approach lies in the details: the Hebrew scribes appear to draw upon all the known codes, which would have required a truly exceptional library at their disposal. A middle approach is to see the law codes as part of an intellectual tradition, part oral and part written, that spread by *diffusion* from Mesopotamia, following the path taken by cuneiform legal documents, while continuing in practice to interact with the law, both local and drawn from the underlying common legal tradition.

An illustration of this interaction is given by Deuteronomy 21:1–9. Where the corpse of a murder victim is found in a field, the law places responsibility upon the members of the local authority, who must undergo an exculpatory ceremony and take an exculpatory oath. Exactly the same oath in the same situation is attested in practice in correspondence from Ugarit in the thirteenth century. The principle of collective responsibility of the local community for unsolved homicides (without mention of the oath) can be traced back further in the law codes: in HL IV (a later version of HL 6) and LH 22–24. There is thus an interplay between the codes and practice that continues over centuries and puts the biblical law into a perspective of great depth and complexity.

B. Mediterranean

The tradition of the law codes is not confined to the ancient Near East. The Mediterranean basin of the mid–first millennium furnishes more examples:

1. The laws of Drakon, from seventh century Athens, with only a few sections surviving in a fifth-century copy, plus a few fragments cited by later Greek writers (see the edition in Stroud 1968)
2. The Great Code of Gortyn, from the city of that name in Crete, dated to the fifth century (see the edition in Willetts 1967)
3. The Twelve Tables, from Rome, traditionally dated to 450, surviving only in later quotations (see the edition in Crawford 1996)

All these codes fit perfectly into the Near Eastern pattern of casuistic formulation of everyday laws. While slightly more distant in content, there are still strong affinities. The law in the Priestly source prescribing that a daughter may inherit where there are no sons (Num. 27:1–11; 36:5–9) is already found in a Sumerian code (LL b) but has an even closer parallel in the Gortyn Code (VII 15–IX 24). The intellectual tradition therefore spread not only into Israel but into contemporary societies elsewhere in the Mediterranean basin.

5. THE LAW CODES AND BIBLICAL JURISPRUDENCE

A. The Nature of the Codes

When first discovered, LH was assumed to have been royal legislation, a codification, or reform. It was subsequently noted, however, that neither LH nor the other codes were ever cited in court or referred to as a source of law. A new theory was formulated, principally by Fritz Kraus (1960) and Jean Bottéro (1987), that LH was an academic document, a product of the scribal school, not intended for citation in court.

The cuneiform scribes of Mesopotamia tried to classify the world around them by means of lists—of flora, fauna, grammatical forms, gods, offices, precious stones. A more sophisticated form of list recorded conditions and consequences: medical symptoms and their diagnosis, omens and their meaning, actions and their legal redress. The latter type of list was cast into the form of objective, hypothetical cases: "If a woman gives birth, and the left foot (of the child) is withered—that house will prosper." The "laws" of LH present just such a list, as do the other law codes. The law codes are thus a product of Mesopotamian science, which is obviously not the same as modern science, but more akin to Wisdom literature.

The process of the composition of a law code was complex. The starting point was a legal case. It may have been a real case judged by a court; it may have been drawn from a well-known incident in epic or historical legend (which was regarded as a factual event); or it may have been a purely fictitious case invented for the sake of argument. Preferably it was a case that involved some delicate or liminal legal point that would provide food for discussion and throw into relief more commonplace rules. The case was then stripped of all nonessential facts (e.g., the names of the parties, circumstances not relevant to the decision) and turned into a theoretical hypothesis, with its legal solution. Details of the hypothetical circumstances were then altered to create a series of alternatives, for example, that would change liability to nonliability or that would aggravate or mitigate the penalty. That series of variations around a single case formed a scholarly problem, which could be used as a paradigm for teaching or for further discussion. Over time, a canon of traditional problems emerged that was passed on from school to school and society to society, over several millennia.

Around the Mediterranean in the mid–first millennium an intellectual revolution began that was to overturn the static world of Mesopotamian science. The science of lists lacked certain analytical tools, making it less effective for expressing legal principles. It compiled only open-ended lists of examples, arranged in groups by similarity. It lacked vertical classification by means of exhaustive categories and subcategories, as well as definition of abstract concepts.

The Greeks, in inventing philosophy, also supplied these desiderata. The new reasoning led to an explosion in legal science and ultimately to the rise of a new profession—the jurist. While the old casuistic method continued to exist in the study of law, as it does still today, it was supplemented by a new way of looking at the law, including the products of the old thinking. Law codes were treated as exhaustive treatises and their text regarded as the ultimate font of law. A new practice arose of citing textual references as authority and a new science of legalistic reasoning.

The composition of the Bible straddles this era of revolution and reflects its tensions. On the one hand, the law codes of the Torah reflect the older

Mesopotamian approach to the compilation of legal rules and traditions. On the other hand, they are presented in a light that is reminiscent of the later, more legalistic approach. That is, the biblical codes are placed in a narrative framework that represents them as legislation given by God through Moses, and they are supposed to be applied in ancient Israel from that time on. In the period following the Babylonian exile, Ezra the scribe and his followers do indeed read and cite them as authority. In the earlier historical and prophetical books, however, the laws are never specifically referred to in any context from the settlement of the promised land onward. Moreover, in structure and content, the laws do not resemble legislation; they are still based on the Mesopotamian science of lists.

The reinterpretation of laws drawn from older sources—that is, the new kind of authority granted to them—that is adumbrated in the last stages of the Bible's composition comes to completion in postbiblical times, when the laws of the Torah were applied in Jewish courts as normative law. The Mishnah adopts and expands the legislative narrative of the Bible, using it as the basis both of the Torah's authority and of the authority of the Tannaim to interpret it (Mishnah, *Pirkei Aboth* 1:1):

> Moses received Torah from Sinai and transmitted it to Joshua, and Joshua to the Elders, and the Elders to the Prophets, and the Prophets transmitted it to the men of the Great Synagogue (Knesset).

By the same token, the intellectual revolution that had begun with the Greek philosophers and had spread throughout the Near East after Alexander's conquest infused the thinking of the Tannaitic jurists and of philosophers like Philo. Their rationalistic interpretation cast a veil over the original meaning of many of the individual biblical laws. Only now, with the discovery of sources from Israel's neighbors of earlier periods are we acquiring the means to lift it.

B. Reading the Codes

In the Mishpatim Exodus 21:28–36 and 22:4–5 present a typical selection of casuistic laws, arranged by association:

> 21:28. If an ox gores a man or a woman to death, the ox shall be stoned, and its flesh not eaten; but the owner of the ox is free of liability.
> 29. If the ox is a previous gorer and its owner is warned but does not guard it and it causes the death of a man or a woman, the ox shall be stoned, and its owner shall be killed.
> 30. If ransom is demanded of him, he shall pay for saving his life whatever is demanded of him.
> 31. If it gores a son or a daughter, the same rule will apply to him.

32. If it gores a male or female slave, he shall pay their owner 30 shekels and the ox shall be stoned.
33. If a man opens a pit or digs a pit and does not cover it and an ox or an ass falls into it,
34. the owner of the pit shall make restitution; he shall indemnify its owner for the value, and the dead (animal) shall be his.
35. If a man's ox gores his neighbor's ox and it dies, they shall sell the living ox and divide its price and also divide the dead (ox).
22:4. If a man has a field or a vineyard grazed and he sends the grazing animals out and they graze another's field, he shall make restitution with the best of his field and the best of his vineyard.
5. If fire goes out and catches on thorns and sheaf, stack, or field are consumed, the one who caused the fire shall make restitution for the burning.

The first selection is a classic scholarly problem of the ancient Near Eastern law codes, organized around the material theme of the ox. The examples follow the associative pattern: ox kills human, human kills ox, ox kills ox. The victims form a subtheme of variants by status: man, woman, son, daughter, slave. A second subtheme is the variant: owner not liable, owner liable.

The rules of the Mishpatim follow the pattern of the same problem in LH 248–52:

> If a man rents an ox and breaks its horn, cuts its tail, or injures its tendon, he shall pay silver amounting to one quarter of its value.
>
> If a man rents an ox and a god smites it, the man who rented the ox shall swear an oath of the god and he shall be freed of liability.
>
> If an ox gores a man to death while it is walking down the street, that case has no claim.
>
> If a man's ox is a gorer and his city council has warned him that it is a gorer but he has not docked its horns or kept his ox under control, and the ox gores the son of a man and causes his death, he shall pay thirty shekels of silver.
>
> If (it gores) the slave of a man, he shall pay twenty shekels of silver.

The organizational principles are the same. The laws are associated with the material theme of an ox: ox as victim, ox as perpetrator, subthemes of nonliability or liability and status of the victim.

The second selection from the Mishpatim consists merely of two examples of the negligent management of a field that results in damage to a neighbor's field. This selection also follows a pattern from a cuneiform code, namely, that of two laws in the Hittite Code (HL 106–7). In the Mishnah, these disparate examples are brought together to form a universal review of the law of damages. Using the tools of Greek logic, lists are turned into abstract categories (*Bava Qamma* 1:1):

> The four heads of damage are: the ox and the pit and the devourer and the fire. The ox is not like the devourer and the devourer is not like the ox, nor are both these, which are living, like the fire, which is not living. Nor are all these, whose nature is to go forth and cause damage, like the pit, whose nature is not to go forth and cause damage. What is the same in them is that their nature is to cause damage and that you are responsible for guarding them, and when they cause damage, the one who caused it is liable to pay compensation with the best of his land.

By turning them into categories, the Mishnah has transformed the legal nature of the examples. They now constitute a comprehensive law on the topic in question. There is no need to look beyond the text constituted by these examples in order to discover the law of damages.

The work of the Rabbis goes further. We are used to the idea of the Bible as a sacred text, but that too was a new idea that arose in the latter part of the first millennium BCE. It was a special application of the new science of legalism, which sees the written law as an authoritative text, in whose words the answer must be found or not at all. This is, in part, why the book of Ezra and other texts can begin citing biblical laws as authoritative standards. Such a legalistic approach continues to develop unabated into the Common Era, and for a legislative text, legalism means that every word of the text is significant and requires legal interpretation. It is the Rabbis who begin to perform this task, and one sees it clearly in the Mekhilta, a Tannaitic commentary on the book of Exodus and the laws of the Mishpatim. In the tractate *Neziqin*, the biblical law of the goring ox (Exod. 21:29) is considered.

> 112–20. *Previously*. One day and another day preceding it and still another day preceding the latter. What is an "unwarned" ox and what is a "warned" ox? A "warned" ox is one about which the owner has been warned three times. Such a one is considered "unwarned" again if a child can safely play with its horns. These are the words of Rabbi Meir.
>
> Rabbi Judah says: a "warned" ox is one about which the owner has been warned for three days; and it is again considered "unwarned" if for three successive days it refrained from goring. . . .
>
> Rabbi Yosey says: even if the owner has been warned about it three times in one day, he is fully responsible for a "warned" ox. And what does Scripture mean by saying "Previously"? Merely that if the owner has been warned about it for three days but not consecutively, the ox is still considered "unwarned."
>
> . . .
>
> 123–26. *And he does not guard it*. This includes the gratuitous bailee. *And he does not guard it*. Adequately. In this connection the sages said: If he guarded it adequately he is free, but if he guarded it inadequately

> he is liable. Suppose he tied it up with a rope and yet it went out and did damage. If it is "unwarned" he is free. But if it is "warned" he is liable, for it is said: "And he does not guard it." And in this case it was not well guarded.

There is no evidence that the courts of the time, when the ancient law codes were being composed, engaged in such close reading, even though it may seem natural to a modern reader. It seems obvious to us, because close reading, with the definition of every word, is the way that modern legislative texts are interpreted. An example taken at random from a contemporary American court shows how close the court's approach is to rabbinic legal science and how far from the ancient Near Eastern science of lists.

> ANTOKU, Plaintiff, vs. HAWAIIAN ELECTRIC CO., INC
> UNITED STATES DISTRICT COURT FOR THE DISTRICT OF HAWAII
> 266 F. Supp. 2d 1233; LEXIS 9504 (United States District Court Hawaii, 2003)
>
> Defendants argue that Plaintiff's negligence-based counts should be dismissed because (1) Hawaii's Workers' Compensation statute's exclusivity provision bars them. . . . Hawaii's workers' compensation statutes contain an exclusivity provision that provides:
>
> The rights and remedies herein granted to an employee or the employee's dependents *on account of a work injury* suffered by the employee *shall exclude all other liability of the employer* to the employee, the employee's legal representative, spouse, dependents, next of kin, or anyone else entitled to recover damages from the employer, at common law or otherwise, on account of the injury, except for sexual harassment or sexual assault and infliction of emotional distress or invasion of privacy related thereto, in which case a civil action may also be brought.
>
> Haw. Rev. Stat. § 386-5 (2003) ("exclusivity provision").
>
> Here, Plaintiff claims that Defendants discriminated against her because of a disability, which originated from a work injury to her lower back. See Haw. Rev. Stat. § 386-3. Indeed, Plaintiff filed for and received workers' compensation benefits from 1998 through 2000 for this work injury. Thus, the court finds that Plaintiff's negligence-based counts arise "on account" of a work injury suffered by Plaintiff. See Haw. Rev. Stat. § 386-5. Accordingly, the exclusivity provision bars Plaintiff's negligence-based counts against Defendants.

So important is the exact wording of the statute that the court's judgment is based upon the interpretation not of any legal term but merely of a prepositional phrase. The statute is a purely secular text. The issue can become even more complicated and contested in the case of sacred texts. Disagreements could arise not only between competing legalistic interpretations but also between different views on the value of the approach itself. Certain teachings of Jesus and his followers, for example, were in part a reaction against the application of legalism, which was perceived as excessive. Nevertheless, it is clear that by the turn of the eras the older approach of the list-making scribes had been forgotten; the new approach was here to stay.

Further Reading

Some titles have been abbreviated; see bibliography for full citations.

Barmash, P. 2004. "The Narrative Quandary: Cases of Law in Literature," 1–16.
Bottéro, J. 1992. "The 'Code' of Hammurabi," 156–79.
Dobbs-Allsopp, F. W. 1994. "The Genre of the Meṣad ḥashavyahu Ostracon," 49–55.
Eph'al, I., and J. Naveh. 1998. "Remarks on the Recently Published Moussaieff Ostraca," 269–73.
Fitzpatrick-McKinley, A. 1999. *Transformation of Torah*, 54–112.
Hagedorn, A. C. 2001. "Utilising an Archaic Greek Law Code for Biblical Research," 217–42.
Horowitz, W., et al. 2006. *Cuneiform in Canaan*, 55–59, 61–64, 113.
Jackson, B. S. 2000. *Studies in the Semiotics of Biblical Law*, 114–21.
Kaufman, S. 1978. "The Structure of the Deuteronomic Law," 105–11, 134–37.
Lemche, N. P. 1995. "Justice in Western Asia in Antiquity," 1695–1716.
Lippert, S. L. 2008. *Einführung in die altägyptische Rechtsgeschichte*, 2–8.
Phillips, A. 1970. *Ancient Israel's Criminal Law*, 1–2, 130–31.
Rollston, C. A. 2003. "Non-Provenanced Epigraphs I," 158–73.
Simon, U. 1967. "The Poor Man's Ewe-Lamb, an Example of a Juridical Parable," 207–42.
Van Seters, J. 2003. *A Law Book for the Diaspora*, 21–22, 29–35.
Weinfeld, M. 1990. "The Uniqueness of the Decalogue and Its Place in Jewish Tradition," 1–21.
Weingreen, J. 1966a. "The Case of the Daughters of Zelophehad," 518–22.
Westbrook, R. 2000. "Codification and Canonization," 33–47.
———. 2008. "The Laws of Biblical Israel," 99–119.

Questions for Review

1. Where in the Torah can one find the Bible's three main clusters of laws?
   a. Exodus 20, Exodus 34, and Deuteronomy 5
   b. Exodus 16–19, Numbers 31–33, Deuteronomy 27–28
   c. Exodus 21–22, Leviticus 18–20, Deuteronomy 15–25
   d. Exodus 25–27, Leviticus 1–7, Deuteronomy 6–11
2. In addition to the law codes, what are the other primary legal sources that can be used from the Bible?
   a. wisdom sayings, judicial speeches, petitionary prayers
   b. precedents, judicial parables, legal narratives
   c. the Ten Commandments, instructions to the priests, royal pronouncements

3. What are the three most important ancient translations of the Bible on which many modern translations still rely in addition to the Hebrew text?
   a. the Septuagint, the Targums, the Vulgate
   b. the Authorized Version, the Sifra, Josephus
   c. the Talmud, the Mishnah, the Tosefta
4. Into what two categories can the legal sources of the ancient Near East be divided, and which of these categories contains the vast majority of the texts?
5. Which of the following statements best characterizes the nature of the law that is represented by the legal sources that have survived from the ancient Near East?
   a. The law represented by these sources changes drastically from region to region and from time period to time period.
   b. The law represented by the sources from Mesopotamia is largely the same from time period to time period, but it differs significantly from the law that is represented by the sources that come from western Asia (e.g., Syria, Israel).
   c. The law represented by these sources shows a great deal of continuity and very little change from region to region and from time period to time period.
6. What three law codes, copies of which still survive today, are older than the Laws of Hammurabi?
7. What is the hallmark feature of the cuneiform law codes, a feature that is shared by much of the content in the biblical codes, as well as by codes from the Greco-Roman world?
8. Does this book draw primarily upon the evolutionary model, the literary model, or the diffusion model to explain the relationship between the biblical and the cuneiform law codes?
9. What is meant by the following sentence from this chapter: "The composition of the Bible straddles this era of revolution and reflects its tensions"?
   a. The laws in the Bible straddle the shift from a more legally systematic approach in Deuteronomy to a more religiously oriented approach to law in the Priestly material of Leviticus.
   b. The laws in the Bible reflect features from the older Mesopotamian tradition of compiling lists, and they also reflect features of the newer, more legalistic understanding of law from the Greek world.
   c. The laws in the Bible have affinities with the system of large, imperial powers that dominated the Late Bronze Age and with the system of smaller nation-states that arose in the Iron Age.
10. How does the approach of the early Rabbis to biblical law differ from how biblical legal texts were likely understood when they were first composed?

Answers

1. The answer is (c). Many of the passages listed in the other answers contain instructions for cultic rituals. These sorts of religious rules fall outside the scope of "everyday law."

2. The answer is (b). It is true that some wisdom sayings in Proverbs and some prayers in the Psalms contain legal language and allusions. Like the brief statements in the Ten Commandments, however, they are not an especially helpful source for understanding ancient Israelite law.
3. The answer is (a). The Septuagint (the Greek translation), the Targums (the Aramaic translation), and the Vulgate (the Latin translation) are the most important. The three sources listed in (c) are early rabbinic commentaries on legal and other texts in the Bible.
4. The first and largest category is legal documents of practice: records of sales, loans, marriages, trials, and the like. The second category is that of the law codes.
5. This book clearly favors (c). The number and depth of similarities across regions and time periods is remarkable—a phenomenon that this book will bring to light.
6. The first two are named for kings: the Laws of Ur-Namma from the city of Ur (around 2100 BCE); the Laws of Lipit-Ishtar from the city of Isin (around 1900 BCE). The third is named for its city: the Laws of Eshnunna (from around 1800 BCE).
7. The casuistic sentence. Most laws are formed on the model of an if-then statement. The protasis (the "if"-portion of the statement) describes the legal situation or problem, while the apodosis (the "then"-portion) provides the required action or legal remedy.
8. The diffusion model. This model assumes an origin for many legal traditions in the Mesopotamian heartland. It then posits a diffusion of these traditions around the ancient Near East through a variety of means, such as scribal schools, trade, and diplomacy.
9. The answer is (b). The form of the biblical codes is patterned after the Mesopotamian science of list-making. But the context that is given to the codes presents them as authoritative and binding.
10. The Rabbis take a very legalistic approach to the texts. That is, they perform close readings of the texts and treat the interpretation of every word as highly significant. This is similar to how modern legal texts are read, but probably quite different from how these texts were treated by their earliest compilers. See the section "Reading the Codes" (pp. 27–31).

2

Litigation

All societies require an organized mechanism for settling disputes and handling problematic disruptions of public order. The societies of the ancient Near East were not unsophisticated in this regard. This chapter outlines ancient Israel's judicial system. It explains what information can be learned from biblical texts and in light of other ancient Near Eastern systems. It also describes the types of evidence that individuals could bring before a court, as well as the suprarational procedures that courts could use to reach a verdict in a trial.

1. COURTS

Courts are a standard feature in the societies of the ancient Near East. The overall pattern is similar throughout, from Egypt to Mesopotamia. Three levels of tribunal may be discerned: royal, provincial, and local, corresponding to the three levels of administration. Administrative and judicial functions were not separated; the same officials were responsible for both.

The king was everywhere the supreme judge, although his judicial activity is better attested in some periods than in others. He could try cases both at first instance and on appeal. There was no formal machinery of appeal from a lower court; rather, a subject would petition the king to redress an injustice suffered by a lower court or official. The correspondence of Hammurabi shows that he could act in three ways in response to such a petition: he either tried the case himself and gave final judgment, decided a point of law and remitted the case to a local court for a decision on the facts, or remitted the entire case to a local court.

Provincial officials, appointed by the king, acted in much the same way, combining judicial and administrative functions. They could have a fixed seat, as in the case of local governors, or be peripatetic. In the Hittite emperor's instructions to the Commander of the Border Guard (*bēl madgalti*), an official with wide-ranging military, administrative, and cultic duties in border territories, the Commander is enjoined:

> When you come to a city, call out all the citizens. Whoever has a claim, decide and make it in order. If the slave or the slave woman of a man or a single woman has a claim, decide it and make it in order. (III 29–32; see the edition in von Schuler 1957)

Whereas the king sat alone and his officials could do so, the guiding principle at the local level seems to have been collegiality. The city council or town elders, however they are described, had judicial functions as a collective body. Most frequently, however, reference is simply to "the judges," without stating who those judges might be. The bench generally consisted of two or more judges and might be constituted ad hoc for the particular dispute. It is a vexed question how far these local courts had coercive powers. At one time it was thought that their judgments were mere proposals for a settlement, but that view has since been rejected. It is clear that the courts had the power to punish and make binding orders. How effective they were in practice is another question. The plaintiff may have had to use self-help just to get the defendant to a local court. It should be remembered, however, that people did not live alone. They were members of families and clans on whom they could rely for support.

A common feature of local courts was that they could be mixed tribunals of local citizens and officials. The *qenbet* in the Egyptian workmen's community of Deir el-Medina is a good illustration, with scribes and other officials often joining the bench. In Mesopotamia, in a case from the reign of Cyrus, the temple administrator of Sippar, another official of the temple, and the city elders sit in a mixed tribunal to decide whether a slave is private or temple property (no. 32 in Strassmaier 1890), while in a property dispute from the reign of Neriglissar, the court is composed of the governor of Babylon, the judges, and the elders of the city (no. 69 in Dalley 1979).

It should not be forgotten that there was a fourth level of jurisdiction. Above kings and commoners alike, the gods sat in judgment. They could be petitioned by anyone, especially if a human tribunal had failed to provide justice. They were regarded by all as a normal part of the machinery of justice.

The biblical situation is usually discussed in chronological terms: while it is agreed that the courts of the monarchical period and Persian period follow much the same pattern as in the rest of the Near East, the premonarchical situation has led to much speculation. The consensus is that in premonarchical Israel the administration of justice was radically different, due to the absence of central authority (Wilson 1980). Assessing the evidence is complicated by the fact that the sources purporting to present the premonarchical period date from much later.

A. The Patriarchal Period

The only mention of a court is Genesis 31, where Jacob proposes a tribunal of kinsmen from both families to decide between himself and his uncle Laban. Otherwise, the patriarchs act rather as monarchs, dealing with kings and rulers on the level of international relations. It is often suggested that the patriarchs were absolute rulers within their own households, with absolute power to dispense justice. In fact, the two texts cited as evidence do not hold up under scrutiny.

In Genesis 16:1–6, Sarai complains to Abram about the conduct of Hagar, whom she has given him as a concubine. Abram hands Hagar over to the authority of Sarai, who treats her so harshly that she runs away. The legal situation is an initial transfer of authority from Sarai, who owns Hagar, to Abram, to whom she gives Hagar. When the gift has bad consequences for Sarai, she complains to Abram: "The wrong done me is your fault! I myself put my maid in your bosom; now that she sees that she is pregnant, I am lowered in her esteem" (v. 5). Sarai then invokes a tribunal, but the court is not the patriarch himself: "The LORD decide between you and me!" (v. 5). Abram's response is to transfer authority over Hagar back to the original owner: "Your maid is in your hands. Deal with her as you think right" (v. 6). The situation is therefore more one of negotiations between potential litigants than an appeal by the one to the absolute power of the other as patriarch.

In Genesis 38, Judah orders the summary execution of Tamar when she is discovered to be pregnant, evidently by adultery. Tamar, however, is not his daughter but his daughter-in-law, and at the material time she is not even living in his house but in the house of her own father. His entitlement to pronounce punishment arises from his standing not as patriarch but as the injured party. Tamar is betrothed to his son Shelah, who is still under his authority and whose interests he represents. There is no trial of Tamar because her family, under whose authority she is living, admits her guilt (given her condition, they could hardly deny it). Again the patriarch's rights are those of a litigant, not of a judge.

B. The Exodus and Wandering in the Desert

The account in Exodus-Deuteronomy attributes to the Israelites a highly organized judicial system, under the leadership of Moses. Moses at first exercises sole judicial authority, but then delegates his powers to subordinate judges. There are three different accounts of the process, which scholars have interpreted as a retrojection of systems from the monarchy. In Exodus 18:13–26, commanders of thousands, hundreds, fifties, and tens are appointed, on the model of royal military organization. The judges are to be able men from among all the people, but in Deuteronomy 1:9–17, selection for the same appointments is less democratic: from among all the "tribal heads." In Numbers 11:16–25, a different system is proposed: seventy elders from "the elders and officials"—perhaps an allusion to the mixed tribunals so common elsewhere.

C. The Period of the Judges

The Bible depicts a loose tribal confederation without centralized courts; legal matters could be resolved before tribal elders at the city gate (Ruth 4:1–12). It was regarded by the biblical author as a time of anarchy when "there was no king in the land and each man did what was right in his own eyes." Using anthropological models, scholars have partially endorsed this assessment. In a system of lineages (clans/sibs) with no central authority, disputes must be settled voluntarily, by a process of arbitration rather than coercion.

Two biblical passages are usually cited in support of this view. Joshua 7 describes the trial of Achan for stealing booty. Joshua persuades him to confess his guilt, which might suggest a voluntary procedure. On the other hand, the process of identifying Achan as the culprit is coercive: each clan, house, and individual is obliged to submit to oracular judgment. The sentence passed on Achan and his family, stoning and burning by the whole community, seems somewhat harsher than would be expected from a voluntary settlement.

In Judges 19–21, the citizens of Gilead, Benjaminites, rape and murder the concubine of a visiting Ephraimite. His response is to call upon the other tribes of Israel to make war on the Benjaminites. There is certainly no judicial procedure, nor is there arbitration; the response is collective reprisal. The legal action taken is a classic instrument of international law, which exactly befits the circumstances of the case. A crime had been committed against a "foreigner" on the territory of another tribe. The injured party could not get justice from local citizens and therefore called in the other tribes. They issued a demand to the Benjaminites for extradition of the culprits:

> And the tribes of Israel sent men through the whole tribe of Benjamin, saying, "What is this evil thing that has happened among you? Come hand over those scoundrels in Gibeah so that we may put them to death and stamp out the evil from Israel." But the Benjaminites would not yield to the demand of their fellow Israelites. (Judg. 20:12–13)

Refusal to extradite was regarded by the other tribes as a casus belli. Clearly, the picture presented is that there was no unitary state with a tribunal before which the aggrieved party could bring his case. Instead, the tribes of Israel, as depicted in the narratives of Judges, formed a classic international community and, in a dispute between citizens of different states within that community, used the conventional tools of international law, namely, extradition and collective security.

D. The Monarchy

The Israelite kings are portrayed as typical Near Eastern monarchs, acting as judge, receiving petitions personally, and presiding over an administrative system wherein officials governed provinces. Solomon is said to have judged from a throne situated in the "courtyard of judgment" (1 Kgs. 7:7). At the same time, the elders continued to administer justice at the local level. Two biblical accounts, albeit somewhat idealized, provide evidence of the monarchic system of courts.

The first comes from Deuteronomy, which sets out a system supposedly to be put in place upon settlement of the promised land. It omits virtually all mention of a king (Deut. 17:14–20 is the only exception), stressing rather the role of the Levitical priests. The system is nonetheless assumed by scholars to be a retrojection of conditions prevailing at the time of the book's composition, namely, the late monarchic period (in the seventh century) and later.

Judges and officers for all the tribes are to be appointed in all the city gates (Deut. 16:18–20). Nonetheless, the elders still preside over local cases, even capital crimes (Deut. 19:11–12; 21:18–21; 22:13–21). The relation between the two sets of courts is not explained, and they may have had overlapping jurisdiction or formed mixed tribunals, as elsewhere in the ancient Near East.

Most cases are to be judged locally (Deut. 17:2–7), but difficult cases are to be forwarded to the central sanctuary, where the priests and the judge preside (Deut. 17:8–13). Note that a single judge is mentioned, implying an appointed official.

The second account comes from 2 Chronicles 19:4–11, which describes a reform carried out by King Jehoshaphat. The king appointed judges in all the fortified towns, that is, on the pattern of provincial governors. He also created a central court in Jerusalem that was a mixed tribunal of priests, Levites, and heads of households. It was to take cases apparently from local courts. There was a division of jurisdiction: the high priest was responsible for sacral cases, and the governor of the house of Judah for matters that concerned the king. It has been suggested that this mixed system reflects Persian practice in the provinces of their empire.

E. The Persian Period

The book of Ezra reports that, in the postexilic community, the Persian emperor's mandate to Ezra authorized him to appoint judges (Ezra 7:25). A great deal of uncertainty surrounds this purported mandate. Scholars disagree over the authenticity of the report in the book of Ezra and over the intentions of the mandate. It is not clear whether the emperor would have wanted Ezra to appoint Persian or Judahite judges and whether he intended that Persian or Judahite law be enforced.

2. PROCEDURE

A. Private Disputes

Legal disputes between private parties were called a *rib* (pronounced "reev"). They had a legal form even in the pretrial stage, and even if they ended in a settlement, without going to trial. The plaintiff might normally be expected to bring the defendant to court (Deut. 21:18–21), but even a local court had powers to summon the defendant (Deut. 25:7–8). In addition, a fugitive could be extradited by the elders of the town where he was to stand trial (Deut. 19:11–13); the P source gives this authority to the "assembly" (*'edah*: Num. 35:12–25; Josh. 20:1–6).

There were no advocates in the modern sense, but sometimes a powerful relative or patron would speak on behalf of a litigant (2 Sam. 12:1–6). God is often portrayed in this role (Isa. 3:13–15; 50:7–8). Otherwise the parties presented their own case and produced their own evidence (Deut. 22:13–19; 1 Kgs. 3:16–28).

While evidence for procedure comes both from the laws and from narratives, the latter present particular challenges. The dispute between Jacob and Laban (Gen. 31) illustrates some of the problems of extracting legal information from narratives. The dispute contains elements of private litigation, but they are difficult to disentangle from the political negotiation between the two sides. Of the two areas of dispute, the first, Jacob's abduction of Laban's daughters, is not presented as a legal dispute but rather as a breach of correct behavior. The second, theft of Laban's gods, is a true accusation that leads to an implicit denial by Jacob, in that he shifts the blame to an unknown member of his household and agrees to their being punished if caught. He challenges Laban to produce evidence by permitting a search. The search, of course, produces nothing, and Laban's legal claim thereby collapses. Jacob's further arguments return to the first, nonlegal theme: the status of Laban's daughters. Jacob does bring up complaints about Laban's breaches of contract, but does not press them as a legal claim; they seem rather a device to gain the moral high ground in the political negotiation.

B. Public Offenses

In crimes like apostasy, blasphemy, sacrilege, and treason, proceedings could be started by a denunciation (Deut. 17:4; 1 Kgs. 21:8–13). The denouncer, sometimes called a *satan* ("adversary, opponent"), stood to the right of the accused (Zech. 3:1). The court could hear evidence from the denouncers, but it also had power to investigate on its own (Deut. 13:13–15; 17:2–4; Josh. 7:16–18).

Such crimes were seen as offenses against God or the king, as the case might be. The offended party, being a figure of authority, could act as both plaintiff and judge, bringing the defendant before his own court. Saul judges Ahimelech for treason (1 Sam. 22:11–16), but note that Jezebel, acting in Ahab's name, brings the denunciation of Naboth for treason and blasphemy before a local court (1 Kgs. 21:8–13).

C. Point of Law

Where the facts were undisputed, the court might still be called upon to decide whether they amounted to a crime or a valid claim in law. In two cases the king is called upon to decide (1 Kgs. 20:39–40; 2 Kgs. 6:25–31). The trial of the prophet Jeremiah likewise turns on an issue of law, which is argued in detail before the court (Jer. 26).

The issue at stake in Jeremiah's trial is false prophecy. Jeremiah has made in public the statements for which he is put on trial, and he does not deny them. The trial is about whether they constitute an offense under the law. The relevant law in the Bible is Deuteronomy 18:20–22, which decrees the death penalty for a prophet who falsely purports to prophesy in the name of the Lord when he has no such mandate.

The argument of the priests and prophets appears to be that Jeremiah's lack of a mandate is self-evident from the content of his prophecy (v. 11). They thereby infer that a "wait and see" test, such as prescribed in Deuteronomy 18:21–22 (if the prophecy is fulfilled, it came from the Lord), would not be applicable. In his defense, Jeremiah asserts his divine mandate and points out that the prophecy is conditional and may be averted by appropriate measures (vv. 12–15). This argument may be an oblique reference to a "wait and see" test. It places responsibility for his prophecy not being fulfilled with the government and people. The elders support Jeremiah's argument by citing a precedent: a previous prophet had made a conditional prophecy of disaster; King Hezekiah's government had heeded him and taken the appropriate apotropaic measures; the disaster was thereby averted (vv. 17–19). A verdict is not explicitly recorded, but the narrative makes it clear that Jeremiah was acquitted.

D. Petition

Aggrieved persons could bypass their local court and petition the king to hear their case and do justice. If possible, the petitioner would try to catch the king's attention by crying out "Save, O king!" (2 Sam. 14:4; 2 Kgs. 6:26; cf. 2 Kgs. 8:1–6). Otherwise, petitioners would enlist the support of a patron at court who would present the case to the king on their behalf (2 Sam. 12:1–6). The only contemporary legal document from biblical Israel, the Yavneh Yam Inscription, is a petition to the local military commander:

> May the official, my lord, hear the word of his servant.
>
> Your servant was reaping; your servant was at Hatsar-Asam. Your servant had finished reaping and had stored [the grain] a few days ago before stopping work. When your servant had finished harvesting and storing a few days ago, Hoshayahu ben Shabay came and took your servant's garment. When I had finished my reaping a few days ago, he took your servant's garment.
>
> All my brothers will vouch for me, all who were reaping with me in the heat of the sun. My brothers will vouch for me that I am truly without fault. . . . [rest fragmentary]

3. EVIDENCE

A. Rational Methods of Proof

Witnesses

The most important form of evidence in a trial was the testimony of witnesses (Heb. *'ed*). It was the parties' responsibility to bring witnesses before the court in support of their case (Isa. 43:9–12).

Objects could also serve as physical evidence in court. According to Exodus 22:12, a herdsman who loses an animal to the predations of wild beasts is not liable to the owner for its replacement. The law requires, however, that the herdsman bring as evidence the remains of the carcass, which the text actually calls a "witness" (*'ed*). In Deuteronomy 22:13–19, a bride's parents produce before the court a (bloodstained) sheet as evidence that she was a virgin on her wedding night. In Genesis 39:13–18, Potiphar's wife produces Joseph's garment to corroborate her claim that he had tried to rape her.

In all these examples the object, even when called a witness, had only limited power to speak for itself. A human witness was required to put the object in context, and ultimately it was the testimony of the latter that the court had to believe.

Most legal transactions were oral and were attended by witnesses, who could be called on to testify in court, should a dispute ever arise regarding the transaction. Boaz gathers ten elders to witness his agreement with a relative over the redemption of family land (Ruth 4:1–11). When the relative cedes his right of redemption to Boaz, he takes off his sandal and hands it to Boaz. This symbolic act is said both to establish the transaction and to be an attestation of it (vv. 7–8), although it is the elders and others present who are actually the witnesses (v. 9). In the future, they may testify that they witnessed the relative's symbolic act of cession.

Notwithstanding the statements of postbiblical authorities such as Josephus to the contrary (*Ant.* 4.8.15.219: "Of women let there be no testimony on account of the levity and boldness of their sex"), women could act as witnesses, at least in court (Deut. 25:7), as was the case throughout the ancient Near East.

An important rule repeated three times in the Torah is that a conviction required more than a single witness. Deuteronomy 17:6 and 19:15 express it as "two or three witnesses"—which is taken by most commentators to mean a minimum of two—while Numbers 35:30 talks of "witnesses" as opposed to "one witness." Since the primary witness might often be the accuser, the idea would be that an accuser should have at least one other person to corroborate his claims. In 1 Kings 21:1–13, two rascally fellows are mentioned as the accusers and witnesses against Naboth on charges of treason and blasphemy. This could be taken as evidence of the application of the law in practice, but many commentators see it as an editorial device to make the story fit the law. Wells (2004) has suggested that the rule was not so rigidly enforced in practice, at least inasmuch as physical evidence might be accepted as a corroborative "witness."

Documents

The huge number of documented private legal transactions from the ancient Near East essentially record oral transactions in the presence of witnesses. A documentary record was not legally necessary, but was advisable where the witnesses' memory might not be reliable. This was especially true of loans, by reason of the large number transacted by a single moneylender and the need to record their repayment or cancellation (easily done by destroying the document), and land sales, which acted as title deeds and had to be durable. There was a possibility that a dispute would arise only among the heirs of the purchaser and seller, when all the witnesses to the purchase were also dead.

The document typically recorded the names of the witnesses to the transaction and in later periods the names of witnesses to the drafting of the document itself. Since a legal document was usually drafted by a professional scribe, there were no signatures. Instead, the obligated party and often the witnesses sealed the document with their personal seal, which could be used to identify them. If only one copy of the document was made, it was given to the beneficiary (the lender or the purchaser). In rare instances, copies were deposited in a central record office, such as a royal archive. These basic practices applied whether the record was on clay, parchment, or papyrus. Documentary evidence, however reliable it might seem, still ranked below testimonial evidence in a court of law. It had to be introduced and authenticated by witnesses and could be refuted by the actual witnesses to the transaction.

Jeremiah 32:9–14 describes an elaborate procedure for providing documentary evidence:

> I wrote a deed, sealed it, and had it witnessed; and I weighed out the silver on a balance. I took the deed of purchase, the sealed text and the open one—the authoritative [version] and the [recital of] terms—and gave the deed to Baruch son of Neriah son of Mahseiah in the presence of my kinsman Hanamel, in the presence of the witnesses who were named in the deed, and in the presence of all the Judeans who were sitting in the prison compound. In their presence I charged Baruch as follows: Thus said the Lord of Hosts, the God of Israel: "Take these documents, this deed of purchase, the sealed text and the open one, and put them into an earthen jar, so that they may last a long time."

The use of a sealed and open version is found in contemporary parchment or papyrus deeds, such as those from Egypt, and continued into the postbiblical period, for example in the archive of the Jewish matron Babata from the Judean desert (second century CE). There is in fact only a single document, but the scribe writes out the transaction twice, with a space in between. The top part of the document containing the first copy is rolled up and sealed and the second half left unsealed. Thus if any doubt arises as to the authenticity of the open copy, the seal can be broken before witnesses and the closed copy consulted.

Presumptions

A device commonly used in the ancient Near East was evidentiary presumptions. Where one state of affairs could be proved, it was assumed to prove a second state of affairs that then determined guilt or innocence. For example, LE 40 reads:

> If a man buys a male slave, a female slave, an ox, or any item of purchase and cannot prove (who is) the seller, it is he who is the thief.

The effect of such presumptions was not to provide definitive proof, but to shift the burden of proof onto the other party. Thus we find in MAL A 14:

> If a man has intercourse with the wife of a man in a tavern or in the square, knowing that she is a man's wife, whatever the husband states is to be done to his wife shall be done to the paramour.
>
> If he has intercourse with her not knowing that she is a man's wife, the paramour is free of liability. The husband shall establish [the case against] his wife and do with her as he wishes.

A man who encounters a woman in a tavern is presumed not to have known that she was married, but evidence can be brought to prove that he in fact knew her marital status.

Evidentiary presumptions are used in the Bible in order to prove a state of mind, when that is an element of the offense. Thus in Deuteronomy 22:23–27, a woman who claims she was raped is deemed to have consented to intercourse if it took place in town and she did not scream for help. If it took place in the country, no such presumption is made, because there would have been no one to hear her cries. The same test is found in a more laconic form in HL 197:

> If a man seizes a woman in the hills, it is the man's sin: he shall die. If he seizes her in a house, it is the woman's sin: she shall die. . . .

Note that Potiphar's wife, in accusing Joseph of attempting to rape her, is careful to establish that she screamed (see Gen. 39:14 and 18, where she instructs the servants in her version of events, which she then repeats to her husband). In Numbers 35:16–24 the type of weapon used in homicide raises a presumption as to whether it was intentional or not.

B. Divine Intervention

Divine aid was solicited to compel testimony. It was generally believed that divine punishment (e.g., illness, crop failure) would fall upon those who failed to confess to a crime or to provide testimony of what they had witnessed. In order to encourage confession and testimony, the Bible provides a system of expiation administered by the priests. Those who did not confess to a crime or lied about their role in a matter of wrongdoing had to make restitution and include a supplementary payment to the victim, as well as bring a sacrifice to the priests (Lev. 5:20–26). Those who should have testified in a case, but did not, had to bring a sacrifice (Lev. 5:1, 5–6).

Where a party did not know the identity of witnesses who might have been present at the events at issue in the case, they could invoke divine assistance. The victim of an offense would issue a public curse on the offender and perhaps on those who knew of the offense and did not tell (Judg. 17:1–3). A curse was a plea to a god to harm the object of the curse in the manner specified. According to Leviticus 5:1, any person with knowledge of the matter who fails to come forward as a witness after hearing a public curse is likely to suffer divine punishment.

C. Suprarational Methods of Proof

A modern court sets standards of proof, such as "beyond reasonable doubt" or "on the balance of probabilities," and if the relevant standard is not met, the claim is dismissed, notwithstanding that there is evidence in its favor. We do not know what standards the ancient courts set, but when unable to reach a decision on rational evidence, they still had recourse to a higher court, that of the gods, through suprarational means such as the oath, oracle, and ordeal, to test the veracity of testimony.

The Oath

The oath was one of the most widespread legal procedures in the ancient Near East. The oath is a curse pronounced upon oneself. An oath can be of two kinds: promissory and declaratory. Promissory oaths are used primarily in contracts (see chapter 6: Contracts).

Declaratory oaths are used in litigation. A declaratory oath is imposed by the court in circumstances where it has decided that it cannot rely on testimony or other rational evidence. The most common form is the exculpatory oath: the defendant denies the accusation in a solemn oath, invoking divine punishment upon himself (or herself: women could also take the oath) if he is lying. It is dispositive, that is, decisive: if the defendant swears, he or she wins the case; if the defendant refuses to swear, he or she loses. Such was the fear of the oath's consequences—divine punishment realizing the self-curses pronounced—that it was not infrequent for the defendant to refuse to swear or for the plaintiff to concede the case rather than let him swear, or indeed for the two parties to reach a compromise rather than proceed to the oath.

The court might impose the oath on the plaintiff rather than on the defendant, or on the witnesses of one side or the other. In the Bible, however, only the exculpatory oath is recorded. The law codes contain three cases.

In Exodus 22:9–10 a herdsman must take an oath regarding losses to the herd with which he was entrusted. The losses could come in the form of death or injury to the animals and possibly also by means of misappropriation, although the text is obscure and its meaning disputed. The herdsman's oath must affirm that the loss did not come about through his exploitation of the animals in breach of his contract. The circumstances occasioning the oath are expressly stated to be the absence of any witness. The oath is by YHWH, but otherwise no details of the procedure are given. The other two examples, however, describe in detail the accompanying ceremonies.

In Numbers 5:11–21 a woman whose husband suspects her of adultery (she is called a *soṭah* in Hebrew) must take an oath to clear herself of the accusation. Again, it is expressly stipulated that there is no witness to her offense, nor was she caught in the act. The procedure takes place in the temple, where the priest prepares a bowl of holy water for her to drink (called the "bitter water of the curse"), into which he sprinkles some dust from the floor. The priest brings the wife before YHWH and causes her to take the oath, reciting to her the curse that will fall upon her if she swears falsely: YHWH will cause "your thigh to fall and your belly to swell." He then writes the curse on a scroll, dissolves the writing in the bowl of water, and makes the woman drink. The exact nature of the curse is a matter of dispute: some claim it means barrenness, others a prolapsed uterus. The most likely explanation is that it refers to a miscarriage, since it was probably the woman's pregnancy that aroused her husband's suspicion in the first place.

In Deuteronomy 21:1–9, where a corpse has been found in the fields, murdered by an unknown assailant, the elders of the nearest village must swear that they have neither committed the crime nor witnessed it. The oath is taken in an uncultivated wadi (where they behead a heifer and wash their hands over it) but is administered by the Levitical priests. Remarkably, the same oath is found in a letter from Ugarit, dating to the thirteenth century (Ugaritica V 27):

> 1–3. Thus says the king of Carchemish to Ammistamru king of Ugarit:
>
> . . .
>
> 40–49. And as regards the case of the woman whose husband was killed together with Hutiya's son in Arzigana, about which you wrote, let the men of Arzigana swear as follows: "We have not killed this woman's husband, brother of Abdi-anatum, nor do we know who killed him."

The Oracle

The use of the oracle in litigation is best attested in Egypt. At Deir el-Medina (New Kingdom), questions were put to the god on a bark carried by the priests. The god would answer yes by moving forward on the priests' shoulders and no by moving backward. In other instances, the oracle "speaks." In the Bible, the nonspeaking version of the oracle is found, with the same yes/no answer. In Exodus 22:6–8, where goods deposited with a bailee have been stolen, the oracle is consulted to determine whether the bailee himself misappropriated the items. In Joshua 7:10–18 the oracle is used to identify the thief of sacred booty by a process of elimination, progressively narrowing the

A SUPRARATIONAL PROCEDURE FROM NUZI (CA. 1400)

One other suprarational procedure is recorded in texts from the site of Nuzi in northern Mesopotamia. For lack of a better term, it is often called the "lifting-of-the-gods" ritual. Scholars have expressed a variety of opinions about it, but the procedure's details are far from clear. One idea is that it functioned much like the oath. Persons told to lift the gods may have actually lifted up divine statues or emblems, while their legal opponents swore by the deities before whose emblems they stood. The text below (no. 108 in Pfeiffer 1932) records a trial between a depositor of goods and the receiver or caretaker of the goods. Even though there are several witnesses who testify on behalf of the latter, the judges still resort to this procedure.

> Zigi, son of Aripapu, entered into a dispute with Ilanu, son of Tayauki, before the judges. Zigi said the following: "I placed thirty seahs [ca. 300 liters] of my barley in the house of Ilanu, and the seals were rolled. I took three seahs of barley from Ilanu, and I demanded the remaining barley from Ilanu. But he will not give it." The judges questioned Ilanu. Ilanu said the following: "Zigi placed these thirty seahs of barley in my house. Zigi [later] took twenty-seven seahs of barley; three seahs of barley from it were left over. Afterward, Zigi took the three seahs of barley that were left over. Then I dragged my hem before the witnesses." The judges demanded witnesses from Ilanu, and Ilanu brought . . . [names of the witnesses] . . . five men before the judges as his witnesses. [They said:] "As for the three seahs of Zigi's barley, his hem was lifted. He said before us, 'I placed my barley in the house of Ilanu, and I took my barley. I also took the three remaining seahs of barley from Ilanu, and I am satisfied.' Ilanu then dragged his hem before us." Then the judges appointed three men . . . [names of the men] . . . as court officers and said: "Go, Zigi, and with respect to Ilanu lift up the gods against his witnesses." Zigi turned back from Ilanu; Ilanu was victorious in the dispute. The judges fined Zigi in the matter of the barley.

While Zigi was the one to "lift" the gods, it may well have been Ilanu's witnesses who were to take the oath. They never get the chance, for Zigi capitulates. Exactly how to understand the actions performed with the hem of a garment is uncertain. This text can also be compared with the law in Exodus 22:6–8, which discusses the possibility of a dispute such as this taking place.

search from tribe to clan to family. The same technique is used in 1 Samuel 14:36–42 to identify Jonathan as the culprit, where it is explained that the people were divided into two units, the oracle decided between them, and then the chosen unit was divided again. The form of the oracle is not given in these sources, but 1 Samuel 14:42 suggests that it was by casting lots. In the latter two cases, the oracle is used only for identification of a culprit; it cannot reveal anything about the crime.

The Ordeal

The existence of the ordeal in biblical Israel to determine guilt or innocence is a much-disputed question. The ordeal is mainly attested in Mesopotamia, in the form of a river ordeal. The accused entered the river and, if guilty, sank below the water; if innocent, the person floated on top of the water. The precise distinction between sinking and floating remains unclear. Sometimes a person who sank was left to drown; sometimes they were pulled out of the water and subjected to another punishment.

The ordeal is not found in any legal passage in the Bible. The procedures for the *soṭah* and the bailee discussed above have been cited as types of ordeals, but without sound justification, since they are perfectly explicable in terms of the oath and oracle procedures respectively. On the other hand, there are many allusions to the river ordeal in biblical poetry, especially in the Psalms (e.g., Pss. 69; 124). They reveal that the concept of the river ordeal was known in Israel, but that it operated purely on a cosmic level, without necessarily reflecting everyday legal practice. Prophetic passages allude to another possible type of ordeal, the "cup of wrath"—a drinking ordeal involving a potion that will be poisonous to the guilty (e.g., Isa. 51:17–23). Again, it is not clear whether this ordeal was used in practice. Attestations of the same practice elsewhere in the ancient Near East are scarce and uncertain.

Further Reading

Some titles have been abbreviated; see bibliography for full citations.

Boecker, H. J. 1980. *Law and the Administration of Justice*, 27–34.
Bovati, P. 1994. *Re-Establishing Justice*, 30–35, 227–30.
Frymer-Kensky, T. 1984. "The Strange Case of the Suspected Sotah (Numbers 5:11–31)," 11–26.
Jackson, B. 2006b. *Wisdom Laws*, 395–430.
Jacobsen, T. 1970. "An Ancient Mesopotamian Trial for Homicide," 196–214.
Mabee, C. 1980. "Jacob and Laban: The Structure of Judicial Proceedings (Genesis 31:25–42)," 192–205.
Magdalene, F. R. 2004. "Who Is Job's Redeemer?" 292–316.
Matthews, V. H. 1987. "Entrance Ways and Threshing Floors," 19/3, 25–40.
McCarter, P. K., Jr. 1973. "The River Ordeal in Israelite Literature," 403–12.
McDowell, A. G. 1990. *Jurisdiction in Deir el-Medina*, 143–79.
McKane, W. 1980. "Poison, Trial by Ordeal and the Cup of Wrath," 474–92.
Phillips, A. 1985. "The Undetectable Offender and the Priestly Legislators," 146–50.
Roth, M. T. 1998. "Gender and Law," 173–84.
Tucker, G. M. 1966b. "Witnesses and 'Dates' in Israelite Contracts," 42–45.
Wells, B. 2004. *Law of Testimony*, 16–29, 50–57, 106–19, 124–32.

Westbrook, R. 2007. "The Trial of Jeremiah," 95–107.
Wilson, R. R. 1980. "Israel's Judicial System in the Preexilic Period," 229–48.

Questions for Review

1. Which of the following best states the four levels within an ancient Near Eastern judicial system?
   a. judges, elders, priests, high priest
   b. village elders, provincial officials, the king, the gods
   c. father, clan leader, tribal chieftain, the king
2. What do scholars currently think regarding the nature of a court's decision in the ancient Near East? Was it a binding decision, an attempt to arbitrate between the two disputing parties, or merely a helpful suggestion regarding a possible solution?
3. Why is it the case that, when Judah orders the execution of his daughter-in-law Tamar in Genesis 38 and then changes his mind, this is not proof that a so-called patriarch was an absolute ruler within his own household?
   a. Judah was not yet head of his own household. He was still under the authority of his father, Jacob.
   b. The right of Judah to make these decisions fell to him only by virtue of his being the victim in the case.
   c. Judah was only one part of a group of elders that were called on to decide the case. He derived his authority from his status as an elder.
4. According to some scholars, the laws in Deuteronomy that say city "elders" should preside over trials were written earlier than the laws that say "judges" should preside over trials. The older system was replaced by a newer one. Why does this book not espouse such a view?
   a. The Hebrew Bible uses the terms "elder" and "judge" interchangeably. It is the very same men who are being referred to by two different terms.
   b. To say that Deuteronomy calls for city elders to preside over certain trials is a mistake. They function in Deuteronomy merely as witnesses or observers of the negotiations that take place between parties.
   c. Evidence from other ancient Near Eastern societies shows that tribunals could be composed of both professional judges and city elders. In ancient Israel, then, both groups could well have had judicial authority at the same time.
5. What is the Hebrew word that is sometimes used for a denouncer—one who accuses another of having committed a serious wrong against a higher authority such as a deity or a king?
   a. *satan* (pronounced "sah-TAHN"—both vowel sounds rhyme with the vowel sound in "John")
   b. *rib* (pronounced "reev")
   c. *'ed* (pronounced like the English word "aid")
6. For ancient Near Eastern societies, what was the most important type of evidence that one could introduce into a trial?
   a. physical evidence

   b. documentary evidence
   c. witness testimony
7. How is the same sort of presumption used in both Deuteronomy 22 and in the Hittite Laws to determine whether or not a woman, who claims to have been raped, consented to the act of sexual relations?
8. Which of the following statements best describes the oath as it was used in the judicial systems of the ancient Near East (ANE)?
   a. ANE systems used the oath as many modern systems do today. All witnesses had to swear by one or more deities that they would speak the truth.
   b. ANE courts, when they chose to use the oath, would normally require it from only one of the disputing parties. If that party swore the oath, they would win the case.
   c. ANE systems used the oath differently from modern systems by having the judges rather than the parties or witnesses take the oath. Judges swore that they would decide the case fairly or be subject to divine punishment.
9. Which type of suprarational procedure is presented in Numbers 5:11–21? Why does the description there not fit the other two types of suprarational procedures?
10. What form of suprarational proof is not found in any legal passage in the Bible?
   a. the oath
   b. the oracle
   c. the ordeal

Answers

1. The answer is (b). The king was the highest human judicial authority, but by means of suprarational methods of proof, courts could appeal to the divine realm.
2. The trend now is to see it as a binding decision. Scholarship is uncertain, however, regarding all of the means that may have been at the disposal of a court to enforce its decision. See the section in the chapter on "Courts" (pp. 35–37).
3. The answer is (b). Judah had a contract with Tamar that she would marry his remaining son. With her pregnancy, it appeared that Tamar had violated this contract, leaving Judah (the other contracting party) as the victim and the one to decide her fate.
4. The answer is (c). Trial records from several different periods of ancient Near Eastern history indicate that judges and city elders, as well as other officials, could preside over trials together. These sorts of "mixed" tribunals were quite common.
5. The answer is (a). This has interesting implications for the beginning of the book of Job, where "the satan" goes before God to accuse Job of having false piety (see Magdalene 2004). It seems quite likely that the author of Job conceived of "the satan" as a kind of job title belonging to one of the heavenly beings that formed the divine assembly. It was

this being's duty—or the duty of whichever being happened to hold this position at any given time—to denounce any suspected disloyalty. The term *rib* means "lawsuit." The term *'ed* means "witness."

6. Witness testimony (c) was clearly the most important. There are a number of cases where either physical or documentary evidence is overruled by oral testimony.
7. Both texts presume that, if a betrothed woman has sexual relations in an urban setting (Deuteronomy: "in the city"; HL: "in a house"), she must have consented to the act and is therefore guilty of adultery. The underlying logic is that, if she had not consented, then she would have cried out for help. Someone would surely have heard her and come forward to testify accordingly. Sexual relations in the countryside (Deuteronomy: "in the field"; HL: "in the hills") do not jeopardize the woman's standing before the law. Her innocence is presumed, since no one would have been near enough to hear her cries.
8. The answer is (b).
9. The text in Numbers 5:11–21 describes an oath procedure. The priest reads the words of the oath to the wife whose husband suspects her of adultery, and she consents to them. In so doing, the woman places herself under the threat of divine punishment. Only time will tell whether or not she will be punished and, thus, whether or not she has told the truth. The other two procedures, the oracle and the ordeal, result in an immediate decision regarding the person's guilt.
10. The ordeal (c) is missing from the Bible's legal passages. It is referred to in other types of biblical literature, such as the Psalms, but most, if not all, allusions to the ordeal in the Hebrew Bible appear to be metaphorical. It is thus doubtful that the procedure was ever part of ancient Israel's legal system.

3

Status and Family

The legal roles of citizenship, gender, slavery, and family are described in this chapter. Readers will learn what distinguished a slave from a citizen, what types of slavery existed in the ancient Near East, and how one could move from citizenship to slavery and vice versa. The chapter also examines the rules that governed various aspects of family life, such as marriage, divorce, and adoption.

1. CITIZENSHIP

In biblical Israel, the criterion for citizenship was ethnicity. The "children of Israel" were theoretically the descendants of a common ancestor, namely, Israel, the other name for Jacob. The genealogical tables of the book of Chronicles purport to trace the distant ancestry of contemporary families, but in practice it was impossible to do so beyond a few generations. Nor was it difficult for outsiders to gain Israelite ethnic identity and with it citizenship, for example, by marriage. Deuteronomy 7:1–3, in forbidding intermarriage with seven named peoples, reveals that it was in principle acceptable. In Ruth 1:16, the widow of an Israelite acquires the requisite ethnicity by a simple declaration of intent. The leaders of the postexilic community did take measures to curb foreign marriages and dissolve existing ones, but it is not clear that the offspring were automatically excluded from membership of the community (Ezra 9 and 10; Neh. 13:23–25).

The legal consequences of citizenship were fewer than today. Public duties like taxation and conscription fell upon the inhabitants of territory under the king's sovereignty, whatever their ethnicity or other citizenship. Apart from cultic regulations, the main effect was in the realm of social justice. Certain laws protecting debtors were restricted to citizens.

A special class of foreigner was the resident alien (*ger*). The term referred to landless foreigners, who are listed alongside the poor, widows, and orphans as deprived members of society (e.g., Jer. 7:6). According to Deuteronomy 24:14, they are entitled to equal treatment under the law, but the laws of slavery discriminate against them. Unlike citizens, they can be purchased as permanent slaves (Lev. 25:47–54).

2. GENDER AND FAMILY STATUS

Special rules applied to women in areas of law like marriage and inheritance and for certain sexual offenses, such as adultery. Otherwise, laws were not gender-specific. Women could own property and make contracts, as exemplified by the woman of worth in Proverbs 31:10–31.

As important as gender, if not more so, was the status of a person within the family. Whether one was the head or a subordinate member of the household made a difference across a large spectrum of laws. The patriarchal household, known as the "house of the father" (*beyt ab*), typically comprised several generations and was the primary socioeconomic unit of society. The head of household was normally a man, who was the archetypal subject and object of the paragraphs of the law codes. On occasion, however, it could be a woman, for example, a widow with young children. For a man, the key distinction was between a son still under his father's authority and a son who had received his inheritance share and was able to form an independent household. For a woman, it mattered whether she was a wife or a daughter.

A wider unit was the clan or lineage (*mišpahah*). Membership entailed certain rights and duties in law. These concerned not only inheritance law but also social justice and criminal law. For example, members of the *mišpahah* were required to buy back ("redeem") real estate or even persons, often dependents of another family, that other members had sold when they had fallen on hard times or accumulated too much debt (e.g., Lev. 25:25–55).

Some passages in the Bible suggest that twenty was regarded as the age of moral responsibility (e.g., Num. 14:26–33; Deut. 1:34–39). There is no evidence, however, of an age of legal majority for the purposes of everyday rights and duties. The question was of less importance than in modern systems, because an adult male would still have the legal status of son during his father's lifetime, while for a daughter the key point of transition was marriage, when she would exchange the authority of her father for that of her husband.

3. SLAVERY

Slaves were property that could be bought and sold, exploited for their labor, and, in the case of women, exploited also for their sexual and reproductive capacity. At the same time, the law recognized the humanity of slaves. For example, they could marry and have legitimate children.

Slaves could be acquired by war (especially women) or be houseborn, but a significant source of slavery, which affected citizens as well as foreigners, was indebtedness (2 Kgs. 4:1; Neh. 5:5). Special laws of social justice sought to alleviate the treatment of citizen debt-slaves and to ensure that their situation, along with their debt, should not be permanent (see chapter 6: Contracts).

The two concepts of a slave, as property and as a person, often came into conflict. The law had no consistent policy, sometimes tending in one direction and sometimes in the other. A slave killed by a third party was treated as a property loss to the owner (Exod. 21:32). The same did not hold true when the owner himself was responsible for harm to his slave. Exodus 21:26–27 makes the knocking out of a slave's eye or tooth grounds for his release.

Some laws represent a compromise between the two concepts. Exodus 21:20–21 punishes the owner whose slave dies as a result of a beating, but not if the slave survives a day or two. A slave who is released by operation of law may take his wife with him, but if it was the owner who gave him his wife in marriage, then the owner has the right to retain both the wife and children of the marriage (Exod. 21:2–4).

Special rules applied to a female slave because of her sexual and reproductive capacity. She could be acquired as a concubine (and retain her slave status), but she could also be elevated out of the status of slave by marriage (Exod. 21:7–10; Deut. 21:10–14). The term "slave-wife" is sometimes used in connection with these unions. A woman could be the slave of one man and the wife of another, or the slave of a man's wife and the wife of her mistress's husband, as in the case of Bilhah, whom her mistress Rachel gave to Jacob as a wife (Gen. 30:4). Nonetheless, the logic of the two institutions argues against the possibility that she could be both the slave and the wife of a man at the same time.

4. MARRIAGE

While the Bible has accounts of people marrying for love, marriage was essentially seen as an alliance between two families. First Samuel 18:22–23 reflects the familial perspective: David is to become Saul's son-in-law, with no mention of the bride. The economic and political implications are spelled out by the groom's father in Genesis 34:8–10, even while proposing a love match:

> "My son Shechem longs for your daughter. Please give her to him in marriage. Intermarry with us: give your daughters to us, and take our daughters for yourselves. You will dwell among us and the land will be open before you; settle, move about, and acquire holdings in it."

For the couple themselves, the most important purpose of marriage was to provide legitimate heirs who would inherit the family property and look after them in their old age.

No law in the Bible deals directly with the central features of marriage. The few laws that discuss marriage are concerned with unusual cases and assume knowledge of the general rules. Several narratives show the practical workings of marriage, but again the cases are unusual or fabulistic. Some information, at least about unhappy marriages, can be gleaned from the metaphor used by the prophets to illustrate the relationship between God and Israel, namely, a loving husband and his unfaithful wife.

Fortunately, the basic principles of marriage law were much the same across the ancient Near East. Copious data from Israel's neighbors therefore provide a solid context into which the scraps of information from the Bible can be inserted.

A. Conditions

A man could have more than one wife. The Priestly source appears to forbid simultaneous marriage with a mother and her daughter (Lev. 20:14) or with two sisters (Lev. 18:18), although Jacob's marriages to Leah and Rachel form an eminent exception. The Levitical rules on incest, which are part of the Priestly source, do not always distinguish clearly between illicit sex and forbidden degrees of marriage. Altogether they appear to be stricter than the rules that were in practice or even than the rules contained in the other biblical sources. They explicitly forbid marriage between paternal half-brother and half-sister (Lev. 20:17, even though contemplated in 2 Sam. 13:1–14) and between brother- and sister-in-law, presumably after the death of the brother, the sister-in-law's husband (Lev. 20:21–22, even though contrary to the levirate law in Deut. 25:5–10—see below).

B. Formation

From the ancient Near Eastern sources we learn that there could be four legal stages in the formation of marriage:

1. An agreement between the groom or groom's parents (sometimes represented by the father alone) and the parents of the bride to give the bride in marriage to the groom. In normal circumstances, this agreement was

a necessary condition for a valid marriage. The bride is the object of the transaction, not a party.

2. Payment by the groom's party of a sum of money to the parents of the bride. The payment is usually designated by a technical term (Sumerian nig-mi-us-sa; Akkadian *terhatu*; Hittite *kussata*; Aramaic *muhra*; Hebrew *mohar*). Payment has important effects on the status of the bride. She is now called a wife, although the marriage is not yet completed, because as far as outsiders are concerned, the marriage is complete. A bridal payment is not strictly necessary but is standard practice for a respectable couple. It creates a stronger form of betrothal.
3. The formal claim by the groom of his bride on the basis of the bridal payment.
4. Completion of the marriage. On this point, the sources are remarkably vague, not making clear what act legally completes the marriage between the bride and groom. Since the bride was already three-quarters married by the bridal payment, it may be that this stage was not regarded as particularly important. There are references to ceremonies and festivities accompanying some of these stages, but their legal significance, if any, is not clear. Marriage was throughout a private arrangement that needed no intervention by state or religious officials, or any other third party.

Stages one and two are illustrated by the HL 28–29:

> If a daughter is *promised* (*tarants*) to a man and another abducts her, when he abducts her he must compensate the first man for whatever he gave; her father and mother shall not give compensation.
>
> If the father and mother give her to another man, the father and mother shall give compensation. If the father and mother refuse, she shall be separated from him.
>
> If a daughter is *bound* (*hamenkants*) to a man and he gives the bridal payment and subsequently the father and mother deny it and separate her from the man, they shall repay the bridal payment twofold.

LE 25 shows the same principles at work in stages two and three:

> If a man claims [his bride] at the house of the father-in-law and his father-in-law rejects him and gives his daughter to another, the daughter's father shall return double the bridal payment that he received.

All four stages are attested in the laws and narratives of the Bible. Genesis 24 details the initial agreement between an agent of the groom's father and the bride's father. Abraham's servant explains his mandate to Bethuel and Laban, the father and brother of Rebekah: to acquire a bride for Abraham's son from among his kin in Nahor (vv. 34–41). He reveals that he has met Rebekah, regards her as the suitable candidate, and seeks Bethuel's and

Laban's agreement (vv. 42–49). They accept: "Here is Rebekah before you; take her and go, and let her be a wife to your master's son" (v. 51).

Neither the groom nor the bride is a party to the negotiations, but there are hints in the narrative that the bride had some right of refusal, at least if it involved going to a foreign land (vv. 5, 39, 55–58). The story makes no mention of a *mohar*, which has led some scholars to suggest that it dates from a late period when the payment of *mohar* was obsolete. The *mohar*, however, was never a legal necessity, and a narrative is not concerned to spell out every legal nicety if it does not serve some purpose in the story. It may therefore be rash to draw conclusions from silence in this instance. On the other hand, participation of the bride's brother as well as her father shows how much the agreement involves the whole family.

The same pattern is found in Genesis 34, where negotiations are opened between the groom's father and the bride's father and brothers. Moreover, the groom himself intervenes to offer a *mohar*: "Demand of me the most *mohar* and gifts, and I will pay what you tell me; only give me the maiden for a wife" (v. 12) . The negotiations are conducted entirely without the bride, who is held captive in the groom's house. The marriage agreement is not in fact fulfilled, due to the brothers' armed intervention.

The story of Samson also illustrates the importance of familial involvement. When Samson sees a girl whom he wishes to marry, he asks his parents to go with him to make the agreement (Judg. 14:1–5). In fact, his statement assigns to them the active role: "get her as a wife for me" (v. 2).

In two cases, the groom negotiates directly with his potential father-in-law. In both, *mohar* is demanded in the form of services: in 1 Samuel 18:22–26, David has to perform an act of military heroism, while in Genesis 29:15–20, Jacob has to work for seven years as a shepherd for his father-in-law. Only then will the second stage of betrothal be reached.

The second stage is easy to identify in the Bible, because Hebrew, like Hittite, has a special term (*'aras*), usually translated "betroth." For instance, a soldier who has betrothed (*'aras*) a wife but not yet taken her is exempted from service in the war (Deut. 20:7). This stage is initiated by payment of the *mohar*. Thus David demands the return of his wife Michal "whom I betrothed (*'arastiy*) for one hundred Philistine foreskins" (2 Sam. 3:14). Hosea, speaking in metaphorical terms, offers as payment righteousness, justice, goodness, mercy, and faithfulness (Hos. 2:21–22). The drastic change in the bride's status is demonstrated by the punishment of the seducer (or rapist) in Deuteronomy 22:23–28. Where the bride is betrothed, he suffers the death penalty as for adultery with a married woman. The betrothed bride is in fact called a wife. Again, this follows the pattern of the cuneiform law codes, for example, LE 26:

> If a man has brought the bridal payment for the daughter of a man and another abducts her and deflowers her without asking her father and mother, it is a case of life; he shall die.

The third stage, claiming the bride, is mentioned once. After working for seven years for his bride, Jacob says to Laban: "Give me my wife, for my time is fulfilled, that I may cohabit with her" (Gen. 29:21). He calls her "my wife" and not "your daughter" because that is her status once the *mohar* has been paid.

Jacob's pronouncement points to the final stage, consummation. In fact, Laban arranges a wedding feast, which is immediately followed by Jacob's wedding night (vv. 22–23). Deuteronomy 21:10–13 regards consummation as making a captive woman into a married woman. Postbiblical Jewish practice eventually takes on two elements: a bridal canopy (*ḥuppah*) under which the groom makes a solemn declaration ("Be to me a wife according to the law of Moses and Israel") and a room into which the bride and groom enter to symbolize consummation (cf. Tosefta *Sukkah* 25b).[1] In the Bible, *ḥuppah* is synonymous with the bridal chamber, where consummation takes place (Joel 2:16; Ps. 19:6). Scholars have also claimed to find forms of a solemn declaration in the Bible, but there is nothing to show that the ambiguous phrases cited are constitutive of marriage. On the other hand, evidence from the Jewish community at Elephantine suggests that the rabbinic tradition does go back to biblical times. A marriage agreement contains the following statement by the groom (no. B3.8 in Porten and Yardeni 1989 = no. 7 in Kraeling 1953):

> "I came to your house and asked of you your sister Yehoyishma in marriage and you gave her to me. She is my wife and I am her husband from this day forth and forever."

The marital misadventure of Samson in Judges 14 and 15 has been variously interpreted by scholars. Some see it as a special form of marriage where the bride stays with her family and the husband visits her occasionally. Another possibility is that Samson was betrothed but left the wedding festivities before consummation because of his annoyance over the discovery of his riddle. The wrong then done to him in giving his bride to his wedding companion (one of the thirty that the Philistines had assigned to him) has a direct parallel in LH 161:

> If a man has had bridal gifts brought to his father-in-law's house, has given the bridal payment, but his wedding companion slanders him and his father-in-law says to the wife's rightful claimant, "You shall not marry my daughter," he shall return double whatever was brought to him and his companion shall not marry his wife.

1. It is not clear when the two elements became separate from each other. The distinction may not have been clear until the medieval period.

The wedding companion in Mesopotamia had something of the role of "best man" and may be connected with the Talmudic paranymph (*šošbin*) who witnessed the bride and groom entering the bridal chamber (Malul 1989). Like the Philistines (Judg. 15:6), the Babylonians took a dim view of the wedding companion marrying the bride, in betrayal of his position of trust, although their solution was less extreme.

C. Legal Basis

A theory of the evolution of human marriage dating back to the nineteenth century saw primitive marriage in one of its forms as a contract whereby the groom purchased the bride from her family. By this understanding, biblical *mohar* was nothing other than a purchase price, as reflected in the common translation "bride price."

The theory, along with the ethnographical approach that produced it, has since fallen out of favor. Paradoxically, it is difficult to maintain for a society that knew ownership of persons. If marriage were synonymous with purchase, there would be no way to distinguish in law between a slave-concubine and a legitimate wife. In any case, the Bible offers no clear examples of brides being purchased. The one text that might seem to support the theory actually proves the opposite. In Genesis 31:14, Laban's two daughters complain that their father has treated them like foreigners: he has sold them and used up their purchase price. They are simply being sarcastic. Their remarks point to another usage regarding the *mohar* (see below).

Although the theory of purchase is no longer accepted, the nature of the *mohar* continues to be a vexed question. It has been proposed that the *mohar* is a mere liberality (Burrows 1938), but a free gift is hard to reconcile both with the radical effects that the *mohar* has on a girl's status, sometimes leading to the death penalty, and with its being the basis for the groom's legal claim to the bride. At the other extreme, theories based on the economic value of the payment, seeing it for example as compensation for loss of the bride's services, have difficulty in finding a market value for foreskins, as in the case of David's *mohar* for Saul's daughter, Michal.

Another traditional view is that it is payment for the girl's virginity. In Exodus 22:15–16, a man who seduces an unbetrothed girl and whose father refuses to give her to him in marriage must pay the *mohar* of *betulot*, often translated as "virgins." It is true that virginity was prized and that a young unmarried girl was assumed to be a virgin, but the term *betulah* does not necessarily mean a physiological virgin, as illustrated by Joel 1:8, where a *betulah* mourns her late husband. In addition, a marriage document from Elephantine (no. B2.6 in Porten and Yardeni 1989 = no. 15 in Cowley 1923) contains a *muhra* paid for a woman who has been married at least once before.

AN OLD BABYLONIAN MARRIAGE CONTRACT

This document (no. 90 in Meissner 1893) records the marriage that was arranged between the groom and the mother (likely adoptive) of the bride. The harsh punishment set forth for the bride, should she choose to divorce her husband, illustrates how severely limited this option was for women, even though it may have been legal, at least in theory, for women to initiate a divorce.

> Rimum, the son of Shamhatum, married Bashtum, the daughter of Belishunu, the priestess of Shamash and the daughter of Usi-bitum. Belishunu has received X [text is illegible at this point] shekels of silver as the bride-payment of Bashtum. Her heart is satisfied. If Bashtum says to Rimum her husband, "You are not my husband," Bashtum will be thrown into the river [to drown]. If Rimum says to Bashtum his wife, "You are not my wife," he will give her ten shekels of silver as her divorce-payment.

The *mohar* creates a right in the groom to take his bride away from the authority of her parents or guardian. It also gives the groom right to sexual exclusivity over the bride as against third parties, even before marriage. And it gave David the right to claim back his wife Michal from her second husband (2 Sam. 3:14–16; see below). Precisely what character these rights gave to Israelite marriage remains an open question.

D. Divorce

In the ancient Near East, divorce was a private, unilateral act. Theoretically, it could be performed by either husband or wife, but in practice it was essentially carried out only by the husband, since in most societies the marriage contract placed heavy sanctions upon a wife who presumed to divorce her husband. The standard form for divorce was a formal declaration: "You are not my wife (husband)." Although immediately effective, divorce involved financial penalties on the divorcing spouse if the divorce could not be justified by some wrong committed by the other.

In the Bible, divorce is mentioned in passing in a number of laws and other contexts, and it always entails a husband divorcing his wife. Nonetheless, it is worth noting that Jewish marriage contracts from Elephantine contemplate the possibility of either spouse divorcing, and with roughly parallel consequences (no. B3.8 in Porten and Yardeni 1989 = no. 7 in Kraeling 1953):

> Tomorrow or another day, if Ananiah stands up in an assembly and declares, "I hate my wife Yehoyishma; she shall not be my wife," silver of hatred is upon his head. He shall give her everything she brought into his house, her cash and her clothes worth seven karsh, eight

> shekels and five hallur of silver, and the rest of her property which is written down—he shall give it to her on a single day in a single installment and she may go where she pleases.
>
> And if Yehoyishma hates her husband Ananiah and declares to him, "I hate you; I will not be your wife," silver of hatred is upon her head. She shall forfeit her bridal payment. She shall place upon the scales and give her husband Ananiah seven and a half shekels and go out from him with the rest of her cash, goods and chattles, worth. . . . And he shall give her the rest of her property that is written down on a single day in a single installment and she shall go to her father's house.

What looks like a formal declaration is found in Hosea 2:4: "she is not my wife and I am not her husband." Another formality mentioned several times in the Bible is a document, a "bill of divorce" (*seper kriytut*) that the husband gives his wife (Deut. 24:1, 3; Isa. 50:1; Jer. 3:8). In rabbinic law this document (called *get* in Mishnaic Hebrew) became the core of the divorce procedure and necessary to its validity, but in the biblical period it may still have had only evidentiary as opposed to dispositive value, because it was likely the formal declaration that made the divorce effective.

If the divorce was due to a marital offense of the wife, such as adultery, the husband suffered no consequences, quite the contrary. Hosea contemplates stripping his adulterous wife of all her possessions and sending her out naked (2:4–5).

E. Remarriage

Leviticus 21:7 and Ezekiel 44:22 forbid a priest to marry a divorcée (Ezekiel adds the widow of a layman). Otherwise, it would appear that divorcées and widows could freely remarry.

A special situation occurs when a man remarries his former wife, whom he had divorced. Hosea 2:4–22 describes a man divorcing his wife because of her unfaithfulness, heaping punishments upon her, but then courting her and remarrying her. Deuteronomy 24:1–4, on the other hand, forbids remarriage with one's divorced wife if there was an intervening marriage. The rationale behind this prohibition has puzzled commentators as long ago as Philo of Alexandria, who suggested that the woman, after being divorced by her first husband, had married her lover and that the first husband, in taking her back, condoned her adultery (*Special Laws* 3.30–31). Modern suggestions are that this prohibition is a deterrent to hasty divorce (Driver 1902), that it protects the second marriage from intrigue by the first husband (Yaron 1966), that the restored marriage made the second marriage adulterous after the fact (Pressler 1993). A passage in Jeremiah, while not furnishing an exact parallel, has been interpreted as demonstrating that such a remarriage was a polluting sin, akin to adultery (Jer. 3:1). A different approach sees the issue in economic terms (Westbrook 1986b). It distinguishes between the termination of the two marriages: the first, ending in divorce for fault, leaves the husband with the wife's property, while the second, ending in death or divorce, leaves a wealthy widow or divorcée. The first husband cannot profit from his former wife's newfound wealth by remarrying her, when he profited from divorcing her by claiming she was unfit to be his wife.

In 2 Samuel 2:12–3:1, a curious incident is related. In the middle of a civil war between David and Saul's son Ish-bosheth, David reclaims his wife Michal, whom Saul had taken from him and married to someone else. Ish-bosheth takes her away from her second husband and sends her back to David.

The legal basis for the return of Michal to David has been explained as deriving from a principle found in several Mesopotamian law codes, for example, LE 29:

> If a man is captured or abducted while on a raid or military expedition and remains in another land for a long period, and another marries his wife and she bears a child, when he returns, he may take back his wife.

David, as an involuntary exile, had a legal claim to restoration of his marriage in spite of a valid intervening marriage (Ben-Barak 1979).

The remarriage of a widow may in special circumstances bring the law of the levirate into play. According to Deuteronomy 25:5–10, where a man dies childless, his brother (the *levir*, from the Latin word for brother-in-law) must marry the deceased's widow. If he refuses to do so, the widow can bring him before the local court and subject him to a humiliating ceremony. In later rabbinic law, the rule was taken to apply to all marriages, but in the Deuteronomic law there is an important condition: "When brothers dwell together." This is a technical term referring to the period after the death of the father when his sons continue to live in undivided ownership of the estate that their father left to them as their inheritance (see chapter 5: Property and Inheritance).

Two other narratives contain different circumstances but the same legal situation. In Genesis 38, Judah has three sons who are still living in his undivided household. When his first son dies, he gives his first son's widow, Tamar, in marriage to his second son; and when the second son also dies, he is supposed to do the same with his third son. Judah the father had authority to command his sons that the court in Deuteronomy can only imperfectly replace after the head of household has died.

The third case, in Ruth 4, is complicated by the presence of a right of redemption, and its connection to the levirate law has been disputed. (There are also problems with the text, which appears to be corrupt.) A father and his two sons all died without his estate being divided, but purchase of the land by a relative somehow creates a duty to marry the widow of one of the dead sons. In all three cases, therefore, the law is linked to the question of inheritance. Its stated purpose is to provide the deceased with an heir, but it has been suggested that a secondary purpose was to provide for the sustenance of the deceased's widow.

F. Special Cases

Captives

Normally a marriage would not be valid without the agreement of the bride's parents, but in war there is no need to ask permission of the enemy. According to Judges 21, the Israelites had sworn not to give their daughters in marriage to the Benjaminites. They then regretted their oath, as it would lead to the extinction of the tribe. They therefore adopted two strategies: (1) to kill, in a town that had broken another oath, all the inhabitants except for unmarried girls, who were then given to the Benjaminites as brides; (2) to allow the Benjaminites to ambush girls of another town during a festival and carry them off. In both cases, a legal trick was used to avoid a binding legal obligation. In the first, the girls are handed over as captives, not daughters, while in the second, a legal fiction of warfare breaks the legal link between parent and daughter.

Deuteronomy 21:10–14 imposes restrictions on the rights of the captor. If he wishes to marry—presumably by force—a prisoner of war, he must allow her to mourn the (possibly fictive) death of her parents and, having married her, may not reenslave her, should he subsequently divorce her.

Concubines

Exodus 21:7–10 regulates the situation of a daughter sold into debt-slavery, but for sexual and reproductive purposes. Scholars have mostly assumed that the purpose of the arrangement is marriage (Chirichigno 1993). Westbrook (1998) regards it as concubinage, in part because the woman is assigned and taken but never specifically as a wife, and the relationship is ended by sale or manumission, not by divorce.

Being intended as a concubine, the woman is not normally redeemable, as would be an ordinary debt-slave. The right of redemption revives, however, if her owner fails to fulfill the special purpose of the contract and does not assign her for concubinage (*ketiv*) or take her himself (*qere'*). Furthermore, he cannot sell her in such a way as to make her irredeemable ("to outsiders" or "abroad"—translators differ).

If the owner assigns her to his son, he must accord her the "status of daughters," which has been interpreted as an allusion to marriage or to a standing within the household until the son is old enough to consummate the union. If he takes her for himself but then takes another (wife?/concubine?), the owner must not reduce her rations (and her conjugal rights, according to the traditional interpretation).

A free woman could also be a concubine (e.g., Judg. 19). She was called a *pilegeš*, a loanword from Greek (*pallax*: girl). The main characteristic of concubinage is that, unlike marriage, it does not produce legitimate heirs. This would appear to be confirmed by Genesis 25:5–6 (see chapter 5: Property and Inheritance).

Little is known of the free concubine's legal status. In different contexts, the narrator in Genesis calls Bilhah, Rachel's maid, the wife of Jacob (30:4), his slave (32:23), and his free concubine (35:22). This last may have been an attempt to mitigate the crime of Jacob's son, Reuben, in sleeping with her.

5. ADOPTION

Adoption was a widely used and very productive legal institution throughout the ancient world. It was employed not only to remedy childlessness but for a wide variety of purposes, including the transfer of inheritance, manumission of slaves, and even commercial transactions. It is therefore surprising that there is hardly any mention of it in the Bible. The two explicit cases both have a foreign setting: Moses is adopted by an Egyptian princess, and Mordechai adopts his niece, Esther (Exod. 2:10; Esth. 2:7). The latter case shows that adoption was deemed valid in Jewish law, at least in the Persian Empire. Evidence from practice in the same period comes from an adoption contract from Elephantine: it is said to be between two Aramaeans, but both have Jewish names, as does the adoptee (no. B3.9 in Porten and Yardeni 1989 = no. 8 in Kraeling 1953):

> Uriah son of Mahseiah, an Aramaean of Syene, said to Zakkur son of Meshullam, an Aramaean of Syene, before Vidranga . . . the commander of Syene, . . . :
>
> [As regards] Yedaniah by name son of Tahwa, [you]r you[th] whom you gave me and wrote me a document thereon, I, Uriah, shall not be able, nor shall my son or daughter, brother or sister, or man, to make him a slave. He shall be my son.

The document records the manumission of a slave by adoption, which was a common practice in the ancient Near East but is not attested in the Bible. If adoption did exist in practice in ancient Israel, it is curious that it did not survive in later Jewish law. Rabbinic law does not recognize the institution at all.

There are a number of other biblical verses that may contain an allusion to adoption. Rachel gives her maid to Jacob in order that "she may bear on my knees and that through her I too may have children" (Gen. 30:3). When the child is born, it is Rachel who names it (vv. 5–6). Jacob declares that his two grandsons, Ephraim and Menasseh, shall be his, like his own sons (Gen. 48:3–5). A declaration of adoption has likewise been seen in God's statement to a king of the Davidic dynasty, "You are my son" (Ps. 2:7; cf. 2 Sam. 7:14; Ps. 89:27–28).

Further Reading

Some titles have been abbreviated; see bibliography for full citations.

Ben-Barak, Z. 1979. "The Legal Background to the Restoration of Michal to David," 15–29.
———. 2006. *Inheritance by Daughters*, 1–10.
Burrows, M. 1938. *The Basis of Israelite Marriage*, 1–15.
Fleishman, J. 1992a. "The Age of Legal Maturity in Biblical Law," 35–48.
Frymer-Kensky, T. 1998. "Virginity in the Bible," 79–93.
Hugenberger, G. P. 1994. *Marriage as a Covenant*, 230–38.
Levine, E. 1999. "On Exodus 21:10, *'Onah* and Biblical Marriage," 133–64.
Malul, M. 1989. "Susapinnu," 241–78.
Matthews, V. H. 1994. "The Anthropology of Slavery in the Covenant Code," 119–35.
Pressler, C. 1993. *View of Women*, 45–62 (restoration); 63–73 (levirate).
———. 1998. "Wives and Daughters, Bond and Free," 147–72.
Van Selms, A. 1950. "The Best Man and Bride," 65–75.
Viberg, Å. 1992. *Symbols of Law*, 77–87.
Wagenaar, J. A. 2004. "The Annulment of a 'Purchase' Marriage in Exodus 21:7–11," 219–31.
Washington, H. C. 1998. "'Lest He Die in Battle,'" 185–213.
Wenham, G. J. 1972. "*Betulah*, a Girl of Marriageable Age," 326–48.
Westbrook, R. 1986b. "The Prohibition on Restoration of Marriage," 387–405.
———. 1998. "The Female Slave," 214–38.
Yaron, R. 1957. "On Divorce in Old Testament Times," 117–28.
———. 1962. *Introduction to the Law of the Aramaic Papyri*, 40.
———. 1966. "The Restoration of Marriage," 1–11.

Questions for Review

1. What does the Hebrew term *mišpahah* identify?
   a. a nuclear family
   b. a clan
   c. a tribe
   d. a group of tribes
2. What two aspects of slavery often came into conflict in the ancient Near East?
   a. that a slave could be purchased and that a slave could be sold

   b. that a slave could be a slave for reasons of debt and that a slave could be a slave by being born to a slave woman
   c. that a slave was considered to be property and that a slave was considered to be a person
3. How does the law in Exodus 21:20–21 exemplify the conflict identified in question 2?
4. When two people married in ancient Israel, what was the most important purpose of their marriage?
   a. to produce heirs who would inherit the couple's property and look after them in their old age
   b. to maintain a strong alliance and friendship between their two families of origin
   c. to love and care for each other as an example to other families around them
   d. to raise children who would worship the Lord and remain loyal to their Israelite identity
5. Under normal circumstances, at what stage in the formation of marriage could a young Israelite woman be called a wife?
   a. only after the full completion of all the stages of the marriage
   b. after the payment of money from the groom or his family to the parents of the bride
   c. after the groom's family and the bride's family reach an agreement that their two children will marry each other
6. What is the typical translation for the Hebrew word that signifies the action of the stage of marriage identified in question 5?
   a. arrange
   b. betroth
   c. claim
   d. marry
7. What formal declaration was typically spoken in order to enact a divorce?
8. In what situation could a man divorce his wife and not suffer any negative consequences?
   a. in any situation; there were no restrictions or conditions on a man divorcing his wife
   b. when a wife had first initiated the divorce but then changed her mind
   c. when the wife had committed a serious offense, such as adultery
9. In Deuteronomy 24:1–4, a certain type of remarriage is prohibited. According to Westbrook, what is the reason behind this prohibition?
10. What is the law of the levirate, and what three biblical texts refer to legal situations where this law is applicable?

Answers

1. The answer is (b). The term is important legally because members of a *mišpahah* had particular rights and duties in relation to other members of their *mišpahah*. These will be discussed in more detail in later chapters.

2. The answer is (c). It was difficult for the law to treat a slave both as a piece of property and as a person, and certain exceptions had to be made.
3. This law shows that a slave is a person, because the owner must be punished if the slave dies directly after a beating. Were the owner to have beaten another piece of property—a clay pot or an animal—no punishment would be called for. The law also shows that a slave is partly property, because no punishment comes if the slave survives the immediate aftermath of the beating. This would not have been true in the case of nonslaves.
4. The answer is (a). This principle applied across the ancient Near East.
5. The answer is (b). Only after a payment of money to the bride's parents could a woman be called a wife. This made her off-limits to other men. Full completion of the marriage typically came later.
6. The answer is (b). A man who had sexual relations with a betrothed woman could be subjected to the same punishments (including death) that a man who slept with a fully married woman was subject to.
7. "You are not my wife/husband." This is the exact counterpart to the statement that typically formed the marriage initially: "You are my wife/husband."
8. The answer is (c). Again, this is true of all societies in the ancient Near East. If the wife had committed no offense, the man would be required to return her dowry (or its equivalent) to her and also, at times, to pay her an additional sum as part of the divorce settlement.
9. In this text, a woman who has been married to two different men is not allowed to remarry her first husband. The reason is that the first husband has already realized a profit from his relationship to this woman. He divorced her for cause—that is, due to an offense on her part. He thus retained her dowry. She was separated from her second husband either by death or by divorce without cause. In either case, she would leave this second marriage with dowry at the very least. For her to remarry her first husband would allow him to take this additional dowry into his assets.
10. The law of the levirate says that the childless widow of a man who had not realized his inheritance and established his own household prior to his death should be remarried by the nearest male relative of this man, normally his brother. This law is set forth in Deuteronomy 25:5–10. It also plays a role in the story of Judah and Tamar in Genesis 38 and in the story of Ruth and Boaz in Ruth 4.

4

Crimes and Delicts

Ancient societies, including biblical Israel, used categories other than criminal and civil in order to classify different types of wrongs. This chapter introduces these categories and identifies the offenses included within each. It discusses acts such as witchcraft, homicide, adultery, rape, theft, assault, negligence, and wrongs against God. The chapter also considers possible differences within the biblical codes and how these might be understood.

1. CLASSIFICATION

Modern legal systems generally classify wrongful acts as crimes and civil delicts (torts) and approach them in different ways. A crime is an act seen as harmful to the whole community. It is therefore the public authority that is responsible for bringing the wrongdoer to justice, and the public interest is served by punishment of the offender. A delict is regarded as a wrong against the victim alone. It is therefore left to the victim to pursue the culprit by legal action, which offers redress in the form of pecuniary compensation.

The legal systems of the biblical world adopted a different approach, which does not fit well into the modern twofold classification. From the different types of redress applied in individual cases, we can discern roughly three categories:

1. Offenses against a hierarchical superior, especially a king or a god, that called for disciplinary action
2. Morally grave offenses against another individual that called for revenge

3. Offenses against the interests of an individual involving less moral culpability, for which the remedy was compensation

In this area of the law, the biblical approach shares the same basic concepts and categories as its neighbors (both in the ancient Near East and in archaic Greek and Roman law), but may in individual cases adopt a strikingly different policy. The uniqueness of biblical "criminal" law is a highly controversial topic among scholars (Greenberg 1960, 1986; Jackson 1975; Lafont 1994).

2. OFFENSES AGAINST A SUPERIOR

These were criminal offenses insofar as the response to them was purely penal. Only in this category of offense do we meet collective punishment.

A. King

Exodus 22:27 forbids the cursing of a leader. In 1 Kings 21:1–16 an accusation is made against a local landowner named Naboth that he "blessed [a euphemism for cursed] God and king." He is condemned to death by stoning and his land is confiscated by the king. A later notice informs us that his sons were executed with him (2 Kgs. 9:26).

Treason, that is, giving aid to the king's enemies, meets with the same treatment. While Saul is pursuing David, he learns that Ahimelech, the priest of Nob, sheltered David and gave him weapons. Saul has Ahimelech and all his "father's house" put to death, eighty-five priests in all (1 Sam. 22:6–19).

B. God

Offenses against the God of Israel that are mentioned in the Bible are apostasy, desecration of the Sabbath, blasphemy, stealing taboo property, and sexual deviance. Of these, the first two are unique to Israel, as are monotheism and the Sabbath, while the others are beliefs that were commonly shared throughout the ancient Near East.

The Israelites believed that God was perfectly capable of punishing offenses against God's self without human assistance. Therein lies the problem: divine punishment could be collective, falling on the whole population in the form of famine, plague, and defeat in battle. For this reason, it has to become a matter for the law courts before it becomes a matter for God. The intervention of human justice is designed to isolate and destroy the offender, so as to appease divine wrath. Thus an incident in the desert is recounted where apostasy by some of the Israelites led to a plague affecting the whole community. The plague was halted by the initiative of a public-spirited priest, who summarily executed one of the ringleaders (Num. 25:1–9). The laws often emphasize communal participation in the punishment, as a means of distancing the community from the offense.

Apostasy (the worship of other gods) was forbidden in the Ten Commandments (Exod. 20:2–5; Deut. 5:6–9). Capital punishment for apostasy is prescribed in various forms: stoning (Lev. 20:2–3; Deut. 17:2–7), impaling (Num. 25:4), and being made "taboo" (*herem*: Exod. 22:19). This last probably refers to the execution of the culprit and his family and the burning of their property, as is prescribed for a whole city that has become apostate (Deut. 13:13–18). At the sacking of Jericho, a certain Achan stole booty that was "taboo" (*herem*), that is, dedicated to God. The result was defeat for the Israelites in their next battle. Achan and his family were stoned and their possessions burned (Josh. 6 and 7).

Blasphemy was essentially the act of putting a curse—or attempting to put a curse—upon a deity. It was the ultimate act of rebellion. To what extent it also entailed making disparaging remarks about the deity is not clear. Blasphemy was punishable with stoning, purportedly established by a legal precedent from the time of wandering in the desert (Exod. 22:27; Lev. 24:10–16, 23).

The *Sabbath* prohibitions give us some insight into the enforcement of such laws in practice. The death penalty is prescribed for work or making fire on the Sabbath (Exod. 31:14–15; 35:2), and a story set during the wanderings in the desert has a man executed for gathering wood on the Sabbath (Num. 15:32–36). Nonetheless, in the period of the monarchy, Jeremiah's vain protestations against widespread flaunting of the prohibition shows that it was not being enforced by human courts (Jer. 17:19–27). In the postexilic period, Nehemiah does manage to enforce the prohibition, but only indirectly, by shutting the city gates against traders (Neh. 13:15–22).

Certain *sexual practices*—namely, incest, bestiality, and homosexual relationships—were regarded as offensive to God and were among the reasons for the expulsion of the previous inhabitants from the land of Israel. Guilty individuals, whether active or passive participants—even the animals involved (Lev. 18:6–29; 20:11–22; Deut. 27:20–23)—were therefore to suffer the death penalty. From the existence of similar penalties in cuneiform law codes, at least for incest and bestiality, it may be inferred that such prohibitions were applied in practice. LH 154 and 157 punish incest with death or banishment:

> If a man has sexual intercourse with his daughter, they shall banish that man from the city.
>
> If a man, after his father's death, lies in the lap of his mother, they shall burn both of them.

As regards bestiality, HL 188 provides:

> If a man sins with a sheep, it is an abomination; he shall die. They shall bring him to the gate of the king: the king may kill him, the king may spare his life. He may not enter into the king's presence.

The Hittite law shows that bestiality was regarded as an offense against the divinity. (The Hittite king was also a priest, whose purity had to be preserved.)

In the Bible, there are discrepancies between the categories of incest in the laws and practices reported in the narratives, where a man might marry his paternal half-sister (Gen. 20:12; 2 Sam. 13:1–13) or two sisters together (Gen. 29:16–29). The biblical provisions may have been stricter than the law in practice.

The biblical text that has traditionally been understood to prohibit homosexual relations occurs in Leviticus 18:22 (cf. 20:13). Most translations render the verse in this way:

> Do not lie with a male as one lies with a woman; it is an abomination.

Some scholars have argued that such a translation misunderstands the context of the Hebrew phrase (*miškabey 'iššah*) that stands behind the words "as one lies with a woman" (Milgrom 2000; Stewart 2000). Most of the sexual acts prohibited in Leviticus 18 and 20 are acts of incest, but the only persons explicitly identified as off-limits are female relatives. Thus it may be that this biblical text, instead of forbidding all homosexual activity, contains a general prohibition on male-to-male incest. That is, it forbids sexual relations with the kinsmen who correspond to the kinswomen already listed (e.g., if your aunt is off-limits, then so is your uncle). One could translate the verse:

> Do not lie with a male reserved for a woman. It is an abomination.

This view, which relies on a complicated interpretation of certain Hebrew expressions, is still in the minority. If the verse is indeed a prohibition on homosexual activity, it treats it as an offense against God. In this respect, it has no counterpart in any of the surrounding societies. There is at most a suggestion in the cuneiform law codes that it was deeply demeaning for a free man to take the passive role in sodomy. According to MAL A 20,

> If a man has sexual intercourse with his companion, if the burden of proof against him [the sodomist] has been discharged by all means, human and divine, they shall have intercourse with him and turn him into a eunuch.

The offense is not homosexuality at large, but putting the victim, an associate of equal status, in the despicable passive role of a woman. Hence the punishment of the offender: to be treated like a woman and turned into a woman (Daube 1986). The biblical verse, on the other hand, in using the term "male," emphasizes that an offense is committed whatever the status of the passive partner.

C. Other

The law also meted out harsh punishment when persons lower down the social order were offended by those still further beneath them. Disobeying the order of the priest or judge in a lawsuit was punishable by death (Deut. 17:8–12). Likewise, a son—presumably a grown son who had reached an accepted age of maturity—who struck or reviled a parent received the death sentence (Exod. 21:15, 17; Deut. 27:16). The parents of a son (again, a grown man, whose responsibility was to care for his parents) who was disobedient, and a glutton and drunkard to boot, could bring him before the local court, where the sentence was stoning by the local townsmen (Deut. 21:18–21). The ox that gored a person, even a slave, was stoned to death and its flesh not eaten (Exod. 21:28, 31–32). Animals were considered capable of crimes (Gen. 9:5–6), but the treatment of the goring ox suggests that its crime was worse than simple killing.

3. SERIOUS WRONGS

In the ancient Near East, serious wrongs such as homicide, wounding, rape, and theft were not dealt with by punishment in the modern sense. Rather, they gave rise to a right of revenge in the victim or his family. Revenge could take the form of death, mutilation, or slavery. The role of the courts was to regulate revenge so that it was commensurate with the crime. Excessive revenge was considered uncivilized, a symptom of the breakdown of the rule of law, rather than its application. The Bible provides the best evidence of this attitude, in the boast of Lamech, who belonged to the wicked generations before the flood (Gen. 4:23–24):

> Lamech said to his wives, Adah and Zillah, "Hear my voice, wives of Lamech, listen to my word. For I have killed a man for a wound on me, and a boy for a blow on me. For Cain shall be avenged seven times, but Lamech, seventy-seven times."

The leading (but not the sole) principle that applied was "talio" (a Latin term meaning "like for like"). Talionic revenge took many forms: the same manner of death (burning for burning), the same type of injury (an eye for an eye), or the same status of victim (a son for a son, known as vicarious talio). Even where strict talio was not applied, there might be an effort to make the punishment fit the crime. For example, a person who steals beehives is to be stung by bees (HL 92), and a prostitute who dares to veil herself like a respectable married woman has hot pitch poured over her head (MAL A 40).

The right-holder could, however, accept a payment from the culprit to forgo revenge, which scholars refer to as ransom or composition. As paragraph 49 of the edict of the Hittite king Telepinu (see the edition in Westbrook and Woodard 1990) succinctly puts it,

> A matter of blood is as follows. Whoever does blood, whatever the owner of the blood says—If he says, "Let him die!" he shall die. If he says, "Let him pay ransom!" he shall pay ransom. But to the king—nothing.

Sometimes the courts also intervened to impose ransom first and to fix its limits, where mitigating factors justified suspending the right of revenge.

Biblical law operated within the same basic framework of legalized revenge and ransom but deviated considerably from its principles in specific cases. A complicating factor is that the biblical sources do not all speak with one voice.

A. Homicide

Biblical law has a technical term—"the redeemer of blood" (*go'el ha-dam*)—for the person who has the right of revenge (Deut. 19:6). By killing the murderer, he is thought to get back for the family the blood that has been lost. The right belongs to the extended family (*mišpahah*), the redeemer presumably being the nearest male relative (2 Sam. 14:6–7). Even a slave who has been beaten to death by his owner is entitled to be avenged (Exod. 21:20–21: if death is a direct result of the beating). Where the victim has no redeemer, the king may act as his surrogate avenger, as David does in having the killers of Ish-bosheth executed (2 Sam. 4:4–12). In the case of Cain, God himself promises to act as surrogate avenger if Cain is killed (Gen. 4:13–15).

The measure of revenge is the slaying of the killer. The Priestly source, in reiterating this obvious principle, associates it with the principle of talio (Lev. 24:17–21). In the Mishpatim, however, where a goring ox has killed a son or daughter, the application of vicarious talio to the culpable owner's own children is excluded (Exod. 21:31). Deuteronomy condemns vicarious punishment altogether, at least where the death penalty is concerned (Deut. 24:16):

> Parents shall not be put to death for children, nor children be put to death for parents: a person shall be put to death only for his own crime.

The condemnation may also apply to collective punishment.

No less than four passages in the Bible discuss the mental element necessary for murder (Exod. 21:12–14; Num. 35:9–29, 31–34; Deut. 19:1–13; Josh. 20:1–9). They all distinguish between accidental and deliberate killing. They appear to be based on a single scholarly problem in which an accidental killer flees for his life to escape the revenge of the victim's family. The solution is to offer him asylum until he can prove that the killing was not deliberate. In the Exodus law, the place of asylum is an altar, presumably in a temple. In the other laws, certain cities within Israelite territory are designated as cities of refuge. The historical books give no hint of the existence of cities of refuge, but the altar is mentioned twice as a place to seek political asylum, with the fugitive grasping its horns (1 Kgs. 1:50–53; 2:28–34).

Once the fugitive is safe, a trial is envisaged to establish whether he had intended to kill the victim. Deuteronomy assumes that the trial will be conducted by the elders of the killer's city, whereas the passage in Joshua has the fugitive standing outside the city of refuge and supplicating its elders, who must decide the question of intention before allowing him entrance. The Joshua text also mentions a trial before the "congregation" or "assembly," though the precise relationship between what the elders of the asylum city decide and what the "assembly" decides is not clear.

If the court determines that the killing was intentional, then the killer loses his right of asylum and is handed over to the avenger for execution. King Solomon justifies the execution of his political enemy Joab at the altar where he had sought asylum by representing it as revenge for two persons whom Joab had killed when army commander (1 Kgs. 2:32–34).

If the killing is judged accidental, then asylum turns into exile. The passage in Numbers, from the Priestly source, sets the death of the high priest as the term of exile: should the killer leave the city of refuge before then, he may be killed with impunity by the avenger. A somewhat different version of this system applies to Cain. Guilty of deliberate killing, God initially sentences him to exile without asylum—which, as Cain points out, is equal to a death sentence, since anyone might kill him with impunity (Gen. 4:11–14).

The reality of the cities of refuge is hard to judge. They are a unique institution, not found anywhere in ancient sources outside of the Bible. The scholarly problem of the accidental killer who is forced to flee is also unique, insofar as it is not found in the other ancient Near Eastern law codes. There is an occasional mention of banishment—for offenses against the gods like incest, though not for homicide—but not in connection with asylum of any form.

In the Greek sphere, on the other hand, flight, asylum, and exile are common responses to homicide. Temples were places of political asylum, while exile outside the borders of the city-state was the punishment for unintentional homicide in the laws of Drakon of Athens. Any killer so condemned who was found in the territory of Athens could be killed with impunity by members of the victim's family. Similarly, Plato proposes a year's exile for an unintentional killer (*Laws* 9, 865–66).

If the killing is justified, then there is no guilt whatsoever and no right of revenge. The example given in the Mishpatim is of a burglar killed when breaking in at night. If the householder kills the burglar by day, however, he is guilty of homicide (Exod. 22:1–2). This case, with its distinction between night and day, is so common in the surrounding societies that it could almost be considered a literary topos. It is found in sources as far apart as the Laws of Eshnunna (13) and the Roman Twelve Tables (I 17–18 [VIII 12–13]):

> A man who is seized in the house of a subject in the house in broad daylight shall pay ten shekels of silver. One who is seized in the house at night shall die; he shall not live.
>
> If he commits theft at night, if he strikes him down, he is rightfully killed. By light . . . if he defends himself with a weapon [. . .] let him cry out. . . .

Two cases in the Mishpatim touch upon indirect responsibility for death and questions of revenge and ransom. In Exodus 21:22–25, a man who knocks a pregnant woman and causes her to miscarry is also punished in some way at the husband's discretion; but as we have seen in the introduction, the wording is obscure, and translations, ancient and modern, radically differ. Parallels in the cuneiform codes impose a modest fixed payment. They also deal with the additional possibility of the woman's death. LH 209–12 reads:

> If a man strikes the daughter of a gentleman and causes her to miscarry, he shall pay ten shekels of silver for her fetus.
>
> If that woman dies, they shall kill his daughter.
>
> If in striking the daughter of a commoner he causes her to miscarry, he shall pay five shekels of silver.
>
> If that woman dies, he shall pay thirty shekels of silver.

This parallel raises the possibility that the "other damage" (*'asown* in vv. 22 and 23) that could occur is the pregnant woman's death, as some of the ancient translations claimed. The other obscure term in the law is *be-flylym* (v. 22), usually translated "according to the judges" but "based on reckoning" in the JPS. The latter is based on a parallel in HL 17:

> If someone causes a free woman to miscarry: if it is the tenth month, he shall pay ten shekels of silver,[1] if the fifth month, he shall pay five shekels of silver . . .

1. Ancient calendars assigned thirty days to each month. For the societies that used these calendars, a woman would normally have given birth during her tenth month of pregnancy.

Attractive as the parallel may be, it is still inconsistent with the husband's discretion mentioned in verse 22 ("shall be fined according as the woman's husband may exact from him"). Mention of the husband raises the whole issue of revenge and ransom, but the terse wording leaves us without answers.

Many other difficulties lie in the application of these parallels, and they also leave many elements of the biblical law unexplained. Unlike the cuneiform laws, which deal with a single blow by a single culprit, the biblical law mentions a brawl between men. How significant is this detail, and what is the identity of the striker or strikers? If the law does consider death of the pregnant woman, then giving a life for life may make sense, but whose life is sacrificed? The culprit's, or his daughter's, as in the cuneiform parallels, or more than one culprit or their daughters, if the mention of a brawl and the plural verb in the Hebrew ("they strike a pregnant woman") carry any weight? And what should one make of the continuation of the talionic formula ("eye for eye, etc."), which hardly applies to the sort of blow that leads to miscarriage or the death of the mother through miscarriage?

The contradictions and obscurities of the law have led some scholars to suppose that it is a composite text that reflects stages of development in the law. Jackson (1975:106) reconstructs the original law along the following lines:

> When a pregnant woman was injured in the course of a brawl, and premature labour was induced, each participant in the brawl was liable (whether jointly or severally) for the consequences to the foetus. If it was prematurely born, he was liable to the husband's pecuniary demand; if it was miscarried, to provide a substitute.

Even further from the conventional translations is Westbrook's interpretation (1986a:67), which rejects the parallels of the cuneiform law codes, tries to account for details of the biblical law that they do not cover, and offers yet another translation of its two technical legal terms:

> If men fight and a pregnant woman is pushed and has a miscarriage, if it is not a case of perpetrator unknown (*'asown*), he (the perpetrator) shall surely be punished as the woman's husband shall impose (ransom) upon him, and he shall pay alone (*be-flylym*). If it is a case of perpetrator unknown, you (the community) shall pay a life as the penalty for a life, an eye as the penalty for an eye. . . .

Even a reader unschooled in Hebrew or in philology can readily see that any translation of the law of Exodus 21:22–25 must be taken as a provisional interpretation and not as a reliable substitute for the original text.

The second case on the topic of indirect death is Exodus 21:29–31, where the owner of an ox that gores a person is liable to the death penalty if he had been warned of the ox's propensity to gore. The death penalty, however, turns out to be entirely different from modern conceptions of that punishment. The alternative of ransom (*kofer*) is expressly laid down: "If ransom is laid upon him, he shall pay whatever is laid upon him to redeem his life" (21:30).

Thus the death penalty is in fact legalized revenge, and acceptance of ransom in lieu of revenge is at the discretion of the redeemer of blood. In the same way, when King David offers the Gibeonites justice for the murders committed by Saul on their people, they reject ransom and opt for revenge against Saul's family (2 Sam. 21:1–9).

The Priestly source, on the other hand, while recognizing the prevalence of ransom, polemicizes against it: "You shall not accept a ransom for the life of a murderer who is guilty of a capital crime; he shall be killed" (Num. 35:31). It even forbids accepting ransom for an unintentional killer to return from exile before the death of the high priest (v. 32).

Priestly texts consider the spilling of blood to cause ethical pollution of the land and its inhabitants (Num. 35:33–34; so does the D source to some extent: Deut. 19:10, 13). It is an attitude that is perhaps closer to Athenian ideas of pollution than to Mesopotamian (*Antiphon* 2C.11):

> Help the dead man, punish the killer, purify the state. You will thus achieve three good things: you will diminish the number of future criminals, you will increase the number of god-fearing men, and you will free yourselves from the pollution which this man has brought upon you.

Since pollution will arouse God's anger and may lead to collective punishment of Israel, it may also be a conscious attempt to assimilate homicide into the category of offenses against God. Nonetheless, this priestly ideology seems to have been far from actual practice. King David pardons his son Absalom and allows him to return from a neighboring kingdom, where he had fled after deliberately murdering his brother Amnon (2 Sam. 13:28–39; 14:21–24). David is at one time king and father of both the victim and the killer, but P would allow no one in these positions to exercise a prerogative of mercy.

B. Injury

"An eye for an eye, a tooth for a tooth" is perhaps the most notorious phrase in biblical law. Repeated three times in the Torah (Exod. 21:23–25; Lev. 24:18–20; Deut. 19:16–21), it is to all appearances the quintessential expression of talionic justice. Nonetheless, the Rabbis interpreted it differently (Mekhiltah *Neziqin* 8 to Exod. 21:24):

> "An eye for an eye" [means] money. You say [it means] money, but perhaps [it means] nothing other than a real eye? Rabbi Ishmael said: "It is stated: 'He who kills a beast shall compensate for it and he who kills a man shall be put to death' [= Lev 24:21]. Scripture draws a comparison between damage to a man and damage to a beast: just as for damage to a beast there is compensation, so for damage to a man there is compensation."

Their interpretation seems strained to a modern reader. The introduction to the formula in Leviticus 24:19 is unequivocal: "If anyone maims his fellow, as he has done so shall it be done to him." Scholars have therefore tended to see the rabbinic opinion as a disguised reform: the revision of a barbaric ancient law for a more enlightened age. It fit in with a developmental view of history going back to the eighteenth century, which saw humanity progressing in stages from unbridled revenge to controlled revenge to court-ordered compensation. This view was reinforced by the discovery of the Laws of Hammurabi, which revealed the existence of an explicit talionic provision hundreds of years earlier than the Torah (196–97):

> If a man destroys a man's eye, they shall destroy his eye.
> If he breaks a man's bone, they shall break his bone.

The discovery of other and even older cuneiform codes, however, which require payment, not talio, has confused the picture. The old developmental view cannot be maintained, although various attempts have been made to modify it (Diamond 1957).

The rabbinical view may not be entirely unhistorical. The Roman Twelve Tables, roughly contemporary with the biblical codes, provides (I 13 [VIII 2]):

> If he destroys a limb, there shall be talio, unless he compounds with him.

If ransom were a possible alternative to talionic revenge, then the approach of the Priestly source in Leviticus 24:19 is understandable. It is the same opposition to payment of ransom that P manifests in the case of homicide (Num. 35:31).

The three references in the Torah to talio all consist of a list of injuries and maimed body parts, with slight variations in detail. Curiously, in none of the contexts in which they occur do they quite seem to fit. In Exodus, the list follows a case involving the miscarriage of a fetus; in Leviticus, that of a blasphemer, in a sequence that begins with the punishment of homicide and compensation for killing a sheep. In Deuteronomy, it supposedly represents the punishment of a false accuser. The overall impression is of an ancient maxim, applied wherever "measure for measure" is to be the standard of justice, whether or not the case involves any of the physical injuries listed.

The biblical lists closely follow the tradition of the cuneiform law codes, which also recite lists of injuries and body parts. The pattern is shown succinctly in LE 42:

> If a man bites a man's nose and severs it, he shall pay sixty shekels of silver; an eye—sixty shekels; a tooth—thirty shekels; an ear—thirty shekels; a slap on the cheek—he shall pay ten shekels.

The slap on the cheek recalls the response of Jesus in the Sermon on the Mount (Matt. 5:38–39):

> You have heard that it was said: "An eye for an eye and a tooth for a tooth." But I say to you, do not resist one who is evil. If anyone strikes you on the right cheek, turn to him the other also.

The lists in the Hebrew Bible do not include a slap. Their discovery in the cuneiform codes' lists confirms the existence of ancient legal traditions in biblical Israel that were not all written down in the canonical text. The "oral law" of the Rabbis had deep roots. As it happens, a slap is discussed in the Mishnah (*Bava Qamma* 8:6).

With the exception of the slap, the talionic lists comprise permanent injuries. What they may have in common is that they were all inflicted deliberately. In Roman law, the list of injuries comes under the rubric of *iniuria*, "insult." Deuteronomy 25:11–12 punishes a woman who seizes a man's genitals with the loss of her hand, even though it was done to defend her husband in a fight. It is not stated whether she caused injury or not. The law evidently derives from a case also found in MAL A 8, where the injury inflicted is the main issue:

> If a woman crushes a man's testicle in a brawl, they shall cut off one of her fingers. If a doctor binds it, but the other testicle is affected by it and becomes atrophied (?), they shall tear out both her [nipples(?)].

The biblical version seems to have shifted the emphasis from physical injury to insult or perhaps to the infringement of a taboo.

C. Adultery and Rape

In the ancient Near East, adultery was consensual sexual relations between a wife and a man other than her husband, regardless of whether the man was married or not. Extramarital relations by a man, for example, with a concubine, slave, or prostitute, were sometimes frowned upon but were not regarded as adultery. Adultery was a complex offense, being at the same time a wrong by the wife against her husband, by the lover against the husband, and by both against the gods.

Adultery is forbidden in the Ten Commandments but without mention of consequences (Exod. 20:14; Deut. 5:18). Two laws in the Torah impose the death penalty for both wife and lover (Lev. 20:10; Deut. 22:22). Other biblical sources, however, present a less absolute picture. The prophets use the metaphor of an adulterous wife to represent Israel's betrayal of God through idolatry, but the penalty is divorce by God, the cuckolded husband in the metaphor: "Because Rebel Israel had committed adultery, I cast her off and handed her a bill of divorce" (Jer. 3:8). Hosea does talk of stripping his divorced wife naked and sending her into the wilderness to die of thirst, but then contemplates inflicting further indignities upon her and ultimately remarrying her (2:4–22).[2] These penalties fit the approach elsewhere in the ancient Near East, where the husband had a right to punish the wife with death if he chose, but could opt for a milder remedy such as divorce. He could even pardon her altogether. The Middle Assyrian Laws tie the fate of the paramour to the husband's exercise of his discretion over his wife's punishment. According to MAL A 14,

> If a man has sex with the wife of a man either in a tavern or in the main street knowing that she is a married woman, they shall deal with the paramour as the man orders his wife to be dealt with. If he has sex with her not knowing that she is a married woman, the paramour is free of liability; the man shall bring proof against his wife and deal with her as he chooses.

In §15 of the same code, where the adulterous couple have been caught in the act and the husband brings them before a court, his range of discretion is set out in more detail but with the same limitation:

> If he seizes them and brings them before the king or the judges, and if the burden of proof against them has been discharged by all means, human and divine, then, if the husband will kill his wife, he may kill the man; if he will cut off his wife's nose, he may turn the man into a eunuch and disfigure his whole face; but if he will let his wife go, he shall let the man go.

The motive of the cuckolded husband in punishing the paramour is revenge, which opens the door to ransom in lieu of revenge. The Gortyn Code from Greece regulates the procedure (II 20–36):

2. Ezekiel 16:37–41 contains an entirely fanciful scenario in which adultery is compounded with murder and the lovers play the executioner. It is uncertain, therefore, to what degree the details described in the text correspond to societal realities.

> If someone is taken in adultery with a free woman in a father's, brother's, or husband's house, he shall pay a hundred staters; but if in another's, fifty; . . . let him [the plaintiff] proclaim in the presence of three witnesses to the relatives of the one caught in [the house] that he is to be ransomed within five days . . . , and if he should not be ransomed, those who caught him may deal with him as they wish.

Proverbs 6:34–35 canvasses the option of ransom, only to warn a potential lover against relying on it:

> The fury of the husband will be passionate; he will show no pity on his day of vengeance. He will not have regard for any ransom; he will refuse your bribe, however great.

Scholars have differed in their explanation of the discrepancy between the categorical imperative of the biblical law codes and the possibility of accommodation adumbrated by the proverb. Some dismiss the passage in Proverbs as depicting an illicit bargain to avoid the mandatory penalties laid down in the laws (Greenberg 1986, Phillips 1981). Others suggest that the laws of the Torah are not as absolute as they look; they should be read in the light of other biblical passages and the laws of Israel's neighbors (Loewenstamm 1980, Westbrook 1990). Still others suppose a historical development away from a discretionary right of the husband to a mandatory death sentence (McKeating 1979).

If there is a contradiction, it would follow the pattern of the Priestly and Deuteronomic sources advocating a more severe approach, on the grounds that adultery, like murder, is a polluting offense against God. The P source regards it as comparable to incest: it pollutes the land and is subject to divine punishment (Lev. 18:20, 28–29). In three narratives, by contrast, there are divine but no human sanctions. In 2 Samuel 12:11, David has talionic divine punishment imposed on him for sleeping with Bath-sheba, the wife of one of his officers: others will sleep with his wives. Bath-sheba herself receives no punishment, human or divine. The patriarchs Abraham and Isaac go so far as to persuade their wives to sleep with another man, which leads to divine punishment for the (unwitting) lover but none for the wife (Gen. 12:10–20; 26:6–11).

The status of the woman was of importance in determining the offense. Deuteronomy imposes the death penalty upon a betrothed woman and her lover in terms that are even harsher than for a married woman: they are to be stoned to death (Deut. 22:23–24, cf. 13–21). In the narratives, Judah pronounces death by burning for his daughter-in-law Tamar, betrothed to his son (Gen. 38:24), but this may also have been a husband's prerogative, assuming that Judah was acting on behalf of his young son. Sleeping with a betrothed slave woman, on the other hand, was not a capital offense, although it required an expiatory sacrifice (Lev. 19:20–22).[3]

The rape of a betrothed woman was regarded as a serious wrong to which the death penalty applied (Deut. 22:25–27). Note that the issue of the woman's consent goes only to exonerate her from a charge of adultery. The offense was regarded rather as against her fiancé. Rape of an unbetrothed woman belonged to an altogether less serious category of offense (see below).

D. Theft

The most common penalty for theft in the cuneiform law codes is payment of a multiple of the thing stolen. LH 8 reads:

> If a man steals an ox or a sheep or an ass or a pig or a boat: if it belongs to a god or to the palace, he shall pay thirtyfold; if to a private citizen, he shall restore tenfold. If the thief has not the means to pay, he shall be killed.

The other law codes and the practice of the Mesopotamian courts did not impose such a harsh fate for the insolvent thief. For theft and similar offenses, the default punishment was penal debt slavery. A lawsuit from Emar documents its practical application with a piquant twist (no. 257 in Arnaud 1986):

> Kila'e stole a slave of Husiri and was caught with that slave. He brought him before the king for trial. The king gave the notables of the town of Shatappi to the oath, and the king said thus: "If the notables swear, Kila'e shall become the slave of Husiri."
>
> But Kila'e was unwilling for the notables of the town to take the oath; he gave his sister Kibian as a slave to Husiru in substitution for himself.

Multiple payment was common practice also in Israel, as Proverbs 6:30–31 shows:

> A thief is not held in contempt for stealing to appease his hunger. Yet if caught he must pay sevenfold; he must give up all he owns.

In the Mishpatim, penalties of fivefold are laid down for theft of an ox and fourfold for a sheep, if the thief slaughters it or sells it (Exod. 21:37). Exodus 22:3, however, provides that if the stolen property, whether ox, ass, or sheep, is found alive in his possession, he shall pay double, as Exodus 22:6 and 8 provide for any stolen property.

3. This is the traditional interpretation, but it is uncertain, due to *hapax* terms in the text (see chapter 1, pp. 19–20). In our view, the woman is not betrothed but is a married slave held in pledge, and it is her creditor who sleeps with her.

The discrepancy between the two measures has long exercised the minds of commentators. Rabbi Akiba thought the thief who slaughters or sells more wicked (Tosefta *Bava Qamma* 7:2); modern scholars tend to see it as a reflection of historical development. Another possibility is that the twofold measure applies to an innocent receiver of stolen goods, not the original thief.

The multiple payments are not fines, since they are payable to the owner of the stolen goods, not to the state. At the same time, they are not compensation, being far in excess of any loss the owner may have suffered by being deprived of his property, even if the stolen property was irretrievable. They therefore look like ransom for revenge, the latter likely taking the form of enslavement. This impression is confirmed by Exodus 22:2, which rules that if the thief cannot pay the penalty, he is to be sold as a slave, presumably a penal debt-slave as in Mesopotamian practice.

Two types of aggravated theft are mentioned: kidnapping and stealing sacral property. Kidnapping meant the stealing of a person for sale into slavery. It was punishable by death (Exod. 21:16). Narratives provide insight into the penalty for theft of sacred objects. In Genesis 31:30–32, Laban accuses Jacob of stealing his household gods and Jacob responds by promising death for the thief. In Genesis 44:1–10, Joseph's brothers are accused of stealing his divination cup. They propose the death penalty for the thief, but Joseph's steward, knowing the cup has been planted with Benjamin, reduces the penalty to slavery.

E. Perjury, False Accusation, and Slander

Exodus 23:1–3 condemns all forms of false testimony, but the Ten Commandments refer specifically to false accusation (Exod. 20:13; Deut. 5:17). Leviticus 5:20–26 deals with the special case of a defendant who has been exonerated by making a false exculpatory oath but later voluntarily confesses to his misdeed. To encourage confession, the law imposes a very light penalty—considering the gravity of a false oath—of reimbursement plus one fifth and an expiatory sacrifice. Another mitigating factor may have been that the law applies only where the original offense was obtaining property dishonestly and not some more heinous crime.

Deuteronomy 19:16–21 imposes the talionic principle on false accusation: "You shall do to him as he schemed to do to his fellow." In Deuteronomy 22:13–21, however, the penalties do not seem to be in balance. A man accuses his wife of premarital infidelity (most likely during the betrothal period). If his accusation is found to be false and malicious, he is whipped, forced to pay 100 shekels to the wife's father, and forbidden from ever divorcing her . If it is true, the wife is stoned to death.

The apparent contradiction has spawned many theories. Some regard it as a simple discrepancy. Others seek to reconcile the two laws on various grounds:

the rule in Deuteronomy 22:13–21 reflects gender inequality in the Israelite legal system; the husband's accusation is not spoken in litigation and is no more than a slander (Pressler 1993). Another option is that the parties are the husband and the wife's father, not the wife. Between the two men the penalties are roughly equivalent: (a) humiliation, public beating for the husband or public disgrace for the wife's father; (b) money, paid either to the wife's father or as compensation to the husband (based on ancient Near Eastern parallels); and (c) marriage/divorce, the permanent solidification or dissolution of the relationship for which the two men had contracted (Wells 2005).

4. MINOR HARM

In this category fell acts that caused purely economic harm or for some other reason were felt to be morally less blameworthy. With their emphasis on monetary compensation, they resemble most closely modern civil remedies.

A. Temporary Injury

We have seen that permanent injury leads to talio. A different order of remedy applies when a man suffers only temporary disability as the result of injuries sustained in a brawl. The culprit is obliged to pay compensation for the victim's medical expenses and loss of earnings (Exod. 21:18–19). This is a standard scholarly problem in the cuneiform law codes, which all have the same approach. Thus HL 10 reads:

> If someone wounds a man and makes him ill, he shall nurse him. He shall give a man in his place and he (the latter) shall work in his house until he is well. When he is well, he shall give him six shekels of silver and pay the doctor's fee.

B. Negligent Damage to Property

Exodus 22:4–5 requires that a negligent farmer compensate for damage caused to his neighbor's crops by letting his animals loose to graze or letting a fire started on his own land get out of control. HL 106–7 contains the same two cases with similar remedies:

> If someone brings fire to his field and sets fire to another's field, the one who caused the fire shall take over the burnt field, and he shall give a good field to the owner of the [burnt] field and he [the latter] shall harvest it.
>
> If a man lets sheep into a vineyard in cultivation and they destroy it, if it is in fruit he shall pay 10 shekels of silver per x hectares. If it is bare, he shall pay 3 shekels of silver.

In the same way, if a landowner leaves a pit open, and an animal falls in and dies, he must compensate its owner for the loss, and he may keep the carcass (Exod. 21:33–34). The same remedy applies when the owner of a goring ox, although warned of its propensity, has failed to guard it, and the ox kills another ox (Exod. 21:36).

On the other hand, where an ox gores another ox without culpability on the part of the owner, the remedy is an exquisite example of equitable justice: the two owners divide the value of the live ox and the carcass of the dead ox (Exod. 21:35). A virtually identical law is found in LE 53—the closest parallel of any biblical text with an extrabiblical source:

> If an ox gores an ox and causes it to die, both ox-owners shall divide the price of the living ox and the carcass of the dead ox.

While fair in principle, the rule cannot be mechanically applied to animals of differing value, as the Rabbis recognized (Mekhiltah *Neziqin* 12):

> In this connection the Sages said: If an ox worth 100 shekels gores another ox worth 100 shekels, or if an ox worth 200 gores one worth 200, the claimant gets half of the living ox. If an ox worth 200 gores one worth only 100, the claimant receives one fourth of the living ox.

C. Seduction

The serious penalties imposed for adultery and infidelity during the betrothal period do not apply to sexual relations involving a daughter who is not yet betrothed. According to Exodus 22:15–16, the man who seduces her must marry her with an agreed betrothal payment (*mohar*) to her father, but if the father refuses to give her in marriage, he must still pay the standard amount of a betrothal payment. Deuteronomy 22:28–29 treats the same offense more harshly: the man must pay the girl's father fifty shekels and marry her, and he cannot divorce her. It has been suggested that the Deuteronomic law applies to rape, but there is disagreement among scholars as to the interpretation. Although the text talks of his "seizing" her, the language is not the same as in the rape of a betrothed woman in Deuteronomy 22:25.

D. Slave as Victim

Whereas the death or injury of a free person leads to talionic revenge or ransom, different criteria apply when the victim is a slave. When the goring ox kills a slave, its owner must pay the slave's owner fixed compensation of thirty shekels, although the ox is still stoned to death (Exod. 21:32).

Exodus 21:26–27 frees a slave if his owner destroys his eye or knocks out his tooth. As slaves were typically debt-slaves, it was the equivalent of paying off their debt. Biblical law is unique in dealing with injuries inflicted by an owner on his own slave, as opposed to injury to another's slave.

Further Reading

Barmash, P. 2005. *Homicide in the Biblical World*, 12–50, 94–105, 154–76.

Daube, D. 1986. "The Old Testament Prohibitions of Homosexuality," 447–48.

Diamond, A. S. 1957. "An Eye for an Eye," 151–55.

Greenberg, M. 1960. "Some Postulates of Biblical Criminal Law," 5–28.

———. 1986. "More Reflections on Biblical Criminal Law," 1–4.

Hoffner, H. A., Jr. 1973. "Incest, Sodomy, and Bestiality," 81–90.

Jackson, B. S. 1972. *Theft in Early Jewish Law*, 1–19, 41–67.

———. 1975. *Essays in Jewish and Comparative Legal History*, chap. 2: "Reflections on Biblical Criminal Law," 25–63; chap. 4: "The Problem of Exodus 21:22–25 (*Ius Talionis*)," 75–107; chap. 5: "The Goring Ox," 108–52.

Lafont, S. 1994. "Ancient Near Eastern Laws: Continuity and Pluralism," 91–118.

Loewenstamm, S. E. 1980. "The Law of Adultery and the Law of Murder," 146–53.

McKeating, H. 1975. "The Development of the Law on Homicide," 46–68.

———. 1979. "Sanctions against Adultery," 57–72.

Milgrom, J. 2000. *Leviticus 17–22*, 1565–70.

Olyan, S. M. 1994. "'And with a Male You Shall Not Lie the Lying Down of a Woman,'" 179–206.

Phillips, A. 1981. "Another Look at Adultery," 3–25.

Pressler, C. 1993. *View of Women*, 22–31.

Stewart, D. T. 2000. "Ancient Sexual Laws," 66–74.

Weingreen, J. 1966b. "The Case of the Woodgatherer," 361–64.

Wells, B. 2005. "Sex, Lies, and Virginal Rape," 56–72.

Westbrook, R. 1986a. "Lex Talionis and Exodus 21:22–25," 52–69.

———. 1988. *Studies in Biblical and Cuneiform Law*, 39–131.

———. 1990. "Adultery in Ancient Near Eastern Law," 542–80.

———. 2006. "Reflections on the Law of Homicide," 158–65, 168–71.

Questions for Review

1. Which of the following wrongs was *not* considered an offense against the God of Israel?
   a. blasphemy
   b. desecration of the Sabbath
   c. bestiality
   d. murder
2. If God could easily punish those who committed offenses against him, why was it necessary for human courts to intervene and punish these wrongdoers?
3. With respect to serious wrongs such as homicide or theft, the victim or the family of the victim possessed a certain right. What was that right?
   a. the right to revenge
   b. the right to denounce the perpetrator before royal officials
   c. the right to banish the perpetrator from the clan or tribe

   d. the right to receive compensation from clan or tribal leaders
4. A famous phrase from the Bible is "an eye for an eye." In HL 92, a person who steals beehives is to be stung by bees. What term is used for punishments of this type?
   a. compensatory punishment
   b. talionic punishment
   c. congruent punishment
   d. vicarious punishment
5. What is the name given in the Bible to the person who has the right to kill someone who has perpetrated an unjustified homicide?
   a. doer of justice
   b. instrument of God
   c. protector of innocence
   d. redeemer of blood
6. An incident of indirect death is described in Exodus 21:29–31: the owner of an ox that has gored and killed a person is liable for the death and subject to the death penalty. To what alternative does the text refer in lieu of the death penalty?
7. What statement attributed to Jesus in the New Testament may well be related to a very old legal tradition that goes as far back as the Laws of Eshnunna?
   a. the statement about turning the other cheek
   b. the statement about treating others as you want them to treat you
   c. the statement about loving one's enemies
   d. the statement about loving one's neighbor as oneself
8. Which of the following statements best describes adultery as it was understood in Israel and other ancient Near Eastern societies?
   a. any instance of sexual relations outside of a formally recognized marriage
   b. sex between a married woman and any man other than her husband
   c. sex between a married person, either man or woman, and someone other than that person's spouse
   d. sex between a betrothed woman and her husband-to-be
9. If a thief were unable to pay the penalty laid upon him—whether to pay back fourfold or some other multiple of what was stolen—what would be the consequence of that?
10. To what does the statement in the Ten Commandments that is usually translated, "Thou shalt not bear false witness against thy neighbor" refer?
   a. all forms of deceit and lying
   b. all forms of false testimony in a trial
   c. specifically false accusation in a trial
   d. specifically false or deceptive business dealings

Answers

1. The answer is (d). A serious wrong such as murder was considered primarily an offense against another individual.

2. Societies such as biblical Israel believed that human courts were necessary in these instances to prevent collective punishment of the entire society. See the second paragraph under the section "B. God" (p. 70–71).
3. The answer is (a). In the case of homicide, revenge extended all the way to taking the perpetrator's life. Monetary payments often took the place of revenge.
4. The answer is (b).
5. The answer is (d). The concept is that the innocent blood spilled by the perpetrator of the homicide has to be redeemed—gotten back—and that the spilling of the perpetrator's blood accomplishes this.
6. The alternative referred to is that of ransom. Instead of suffering the death penalty, guilty parties can ransom their life by means of a payment of money. Thus one can say that the two principal alternatives that arise in these situations are revenge and ransom.
7. The answer is (a). A slap on the cheek is referred to in LE and in the Mishnah. This tradition evidently existed in ancient Israel but did not find its way into the written law codes of the Bible.
8. The answer is (b). Sex between a betrothed woman and any man other than her husband-to-be is often classified by scholars as adultery as well, since the penalty for this could be just as severe.
9. The thief would be sold as a slave (Exod. 22:2). Presumably, the victim of the theft would receive the revenue.
10. The answer is (c), specifically false accusation in a trial, that is, the accusation that would typically begin a trial.

5

Property and Inheritance

Issues of property and ownership in Israel and the ancient Near East were often connected to questions of inheritance. This chapter explores both topics, introducing concepts important for understanding how land could be acquired and passed down through generations. It analyzes who could inherit in biblical Israel, how wives and daughters were treated in this regard, and how male heads of household had the right, at times, to alter customary practice.

1. TENURE

Kings had the right to confiscate land belonging to a traitor, and by the same token they could give land to a loyal servant. The prophet Samuel refers cynically to this practice when urging the Israelites not to adopt monarchy as their system of government, in imitation of their neighbors: "He will seize your choice fields, vineyards, and olive groves, and give them to his courtiers" (1 Sam. 8:14). The prophet's negative opinion is reinforced by the practical example of King David, who first grants land to Mephibosheth, the grandson of his enemy, Saul, as an act of clemency. When Mephibosheth's servant Ziba informs David of Mephibosheth's treason, David transfers the land to Ziba, but after Mephibosheth himself turns up to protest his innocence, David divides the land between the two of them (2 Sam. 9:9–10; 16:1–4; 19:25–30).

A ruler would also grant enemy land, before or after conquest, for services in the war. Moses, at God's behest, gave land in Canaan to a foreign ally of Israel, Caleb the Kenizzite (Josh. 14:6–14).

The most striking example of a royal land grant is that of the promised land by God to the Israelites. The grant was originally made to Abram in return for his loyalty (Gen. 12:1–4; 13:14–15), then renewed to Isaac and Jacob in turn (26:1–3; 28:13), although it was left to the descendants of Jacob to take possession. A stated consequence of tenure of the land by divine grant is that it may not be sold irredeemably (Lev. 25:23–24). Apart from the right of redemption, agricultural land sold is to return to its original owner by automatic process of law in the jubilee year (see chapter 6: Contracts).

Ownership of agricultural land carried with it certain obligations. A 10 percent royal tax in the form of a tithe (*ma'aśer*) of its produce is mentioned in Samuel's antimonarchic oration: "He will take a tenth part of your grain and vintage and give it to his eunuchs and courtiers. . . . He will take a tenth part of your flocks" (1 Sam. 8:15, 17). No further regulation of this tax is mentioned in the Bible, but there is archaeological evidence of appropriations of agricultural supplies for royal use (Dearman 1988).

What the Bible does regulate is a tithe due to temple personnel. In the P source, this goes to the Levites, who are landless (Lev. 27:30–33). They in turn offer one tenth of what they have received (a "tithe of the tithe"; Num. 18:26) for the benefit of the priests (Num. 18:20–32). In the D source, the tithe is to be consumed by the landowner's family as a sacrificial meal for two years out of three, but in the third to be given to the Levites and the landless: the resident alien (*ger*), widow, and orphan (Deut. 12:17–19; 14:22–29). Both systems appear to be adaptations of a traditional tax. According to Nehemiah 10:38–40, the Levites acted as tax gatherers for the Jerusalem temple, under the supervision of a priest.

The firstfruits (*bikkurim*) also constituted a land tax in the form of an unspecified portion of the harvest. They were expressly designed for the support of the priests (e.g., Exod. 23:19; Deut. 26:1–3; Neh. 10:36–37). No enforcement procedures are mentioned for either tax; Malachi complains that people are defrauding God by not bringing their tithes to the temple, but the only response is the promise of divine bounty for performing the duty (Mal. 3:8–11). Nonetheless, these duties were treated seriously by the rabbinic jurists, who devoted tractates to them in the Mishnah and the Jerusalem Talmud (*Ma'aserot*, *Bikkurim*).

Social welfare measures also imposed obligations on landowners. It was customary for the poor to glean behind the harvesters, but it did not amount to a right (Ruth 2:2–9). Landowners are ordered to leave gleanings for the poor when harvesting, but this seems to be no more than moral exhortation based on a voluntary custom (Lev. 19:9–10; 23:22; Deut. 24:19–21). This seems to apply as well to the gloss of Exodus 23:10–11 on the sabbatical fallow year, that it is for the benefit of the poor. (The Priestly sabbatical and jubilee years have no such rider.) The parallel duty of leaving the corners of the field unharvested may have been a more enforceable obligation, since there were more tangible criteria by which to assess adherence to this rule (Lev. 19:9; 23:22). Like the agricultural tithes and firstfruits, the tractate *Peah*, versions of which are found in the Mishnah, the Tosefta, and the Jerusalem Talmud, was devoted to legal obligations arising from these two customs, primarily the latter.

2. INHERITANCE

A. "House of the Father"

Inheritance is another institution whose basic system was the same throughout the ancient world. On the death of the head of the patriarchal household, the legitimate heirs automatically acquired ownership of the family estate, which they held jointly until they decided to divide, thereby creating new independent households.

Regions and individual legal systems differed greatly in the details. For the societies of western Asia, legitimate heirs meant the legitimate sons of the deceased, with daughters and wives appearing only in special circumstances. Women in principle received their share of the family property in the form of a dowry, which was subject to its own rules. In Egypt and the rest of the Mediterranean basin, daughters were sometimes accepted as legitimate heirs alongside sons, even if they did not always receive equal shares, and they could also receive a dowry. The Gortyn Code, for example, gives daughters inheriting alongside their brothers only half the share of sons, leaving room for additional dowry.

In principle, inheritance shares were equal, but many systems, especially in western Asia, awarded the firstborn son an extra portion. Local custom might accord the firstborn other privileges, such as the right to first choice among the inheritance shares.

Division would usually take place immediately after the father's death. Immediate division might be inconvenient, however, if some of the sons, for example, were still young and unable to manage their own property. Since it was the heirs' decision, division could be postponed, sometimes for many years.

Postponement created a curious legal situation. All the heirs remained joint owners of the land; theoretically each owned the whole property, but at the same time he could not point to any particular field and say, "That is mine." The "house of the father" was artificially preserved as a single unit after his death. Gaius, a Roman jurist of the second century CE, records the peculiarities of what for him was a defunct institution of archaic Roman law (*Institutes* 3.154a and b; see the edition in de Zulueta 1951):

> But there is another kind of partnership special to Roman citizens. For at one time, when a father died, between his legitimate heirs there was a certain partnership at the same time of positive and natural law, which was called *ercto non cito*, meaning undivided ownership. . . . Now in this kind of partnership there was this peculiarity, that even one of its members by freeing a slave held in common made him free . . . and also one member by selling a thing held in common made it the property of the person receiving it.

Unbeknownst to Gaius, this "partnership" was not special to Roman citizens but widespread through the ancient world. It gave rise to all manner of jurisprudential problems that were of particular interest to the compilers of law codes. Their approach is exemplified by two examples. LE 16 rules:

> A loan of fungibles shall not be given to an undivided son or to a slave.

The problem that the law is addressing arises when the undivided son defaults on the loan and the creditor wishes to take back his property. A loan of fungibles (like silver or grain) is paid back not with the exact items lent but only with the same kind and quantity, which may be drawn from the debtor's assets. Because the indebted brother theoretically owns everything, if the debt were large enough, the creditor could theoretically take the whole estate, including the other brothers' potential shares. The purpose of this law is thus to prevent a spendthrift brother from ruining the others.

MAL B 3 deals with an entirely different question:

> If one of undivided brothers utters treason or is a fugitive, the king may do as he pleases in respect to his inheritance-share.

The normal rule is that a traitor loses not only his life; his property is also forfeited to the king. From the point of view of undivided brothers, that would be unfair, since the whole estate would be lost. The king therefore confines his rights to the traitor's share. He can force a division and take one share, or possibly he could leave the innocent brothers to divide the whole estate between them. In either case, the traitor will lose his inheritance.

Division of the inheritance was theoretically a joint decision of the heirs, although failure to agree might lead to litigation. The heirs divided the estate into parcels of equal value, and they each took one share (or an extra share for the firstborn), for which they usually cast lots. Various methods were employed to ensure that the division was fair. In Babylonia, the act of dividing the estate was the responsibility of the eldest; if the others accepted his division, they took an oath discharging him from responsibility. If they quarreled, a public official could be asked to make the division. In Assyria, for certain types of land, an elegant method of checks and balances was employed (MAL B 1):

> If brothers divide the estate of their father, the eldest brother will select and take two shares of the orchards and wells on the land, and thereafter his brothers will divide and take. As regards the arable [?] land and the appurtenances thereto, the youngest brother will sketch out shares, the eldest brother will select and take one share and cast lots with his brothers for his second share.

Management of the undivided estate could obviously lead to conflict between brothers. Gaius's account above reveals a somewhat anarchic situation, although the law codes do contain a few measures to resolve certain types of dispute. In Egypt, to avoid quarrels, one of the heirs, usually the firstborn, might be appointed as administrator (*rwd*) of the joint estate, by the father in a testament or by a court order. Just as the "father's house" continued in law, so the administrator assumed the role of the father in the undivided household.

The biblical passages that touch upon inheritance take for granted the basic system as outlined above. The laws deal with special cases, making adjustments to details, while the nonlegal contexts apply customary principles either literally or figuratively. The biblical system of inheritance follows the western Asiatic pattern, in which sons are the primary heirs and daughters inherit only in special circumstances. Job receives special mention because he gave his three beautiful daughters inheritance shares among their brothers (Job 42:15). The implication is that the daughters would not automatically have inherited along with the sons.

"How good and pleasant it is that brothers dwell together" (Ps. 133:1). With these noble sentiments, the psalmist is alluding to the political unity of the tribes of Israel (Berlin 1987). The image is made more powerful, however, by the use of a technical legal term: "dwell together." It is a reference to the legal institution of undivided inheritance, through which brothers can retain the integrity of the patriarchal family after the death of their father. An actual example of undivided heirs is the community of priests at Nob. Although under the leadership of a certain Ahimelech, the whole community is called his "father's house" (1 Sam. 22:9–16). Priestly offices could be inherited like land or other property. The reference is thus to an office that its priestly heirs had continued to hold in common, perhaps for generations.

The provisions of the Deuteronomic levirate law, in which a man is obliged to marry his deceased brother's widow, are said to apply "when brothers dwell together" (Deut. 25:5–6). The connection with succession becomes clear with the declared purpose of the rule: to provide an heir for the deceased (Westbrook 1991). Two narratives also refer to the levirate in practice. It is not, however, performed by a brother, but by another relative. This has led to much speculation about contradictions or developments in the law, but all three passages have in common the provision of an heir for a man who died while in fact still living in an undivided household (Gen. 38: Er; Ruth 1:14 and 4:1–5: Mahlon). They therefore reveal to us the legal significance of the period of undivided inheritance, even if the intricacies of the levirate law remain a matter of dispute.

The Deuteronomic law is just another example of those paragraphs we have seen in the cuneiform law codes dealing with some special problem that arises from undivided ownership of the inheritance. The problem in this case is connected with the curious fiction of levirate marriage.

Supposing three brothers divide an inheritance, and then one dies childless, who will inherit his share? The other two brothers. But in the title deed to the land, the childless brother (brother A) will at least appear as a past owner. The family tree will look like this:

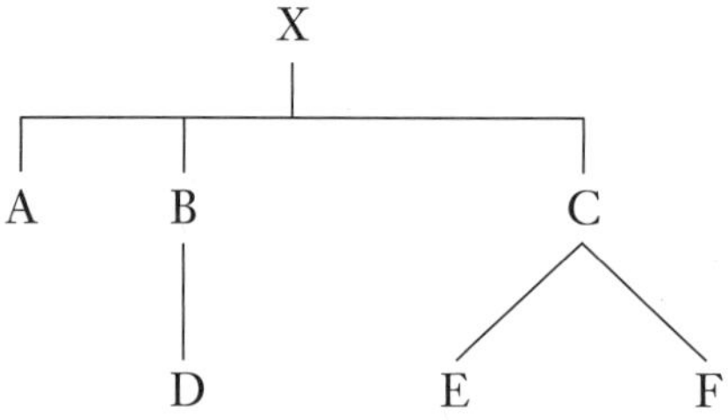

A later title deed to the land that A owned in his lifetime will look like this:

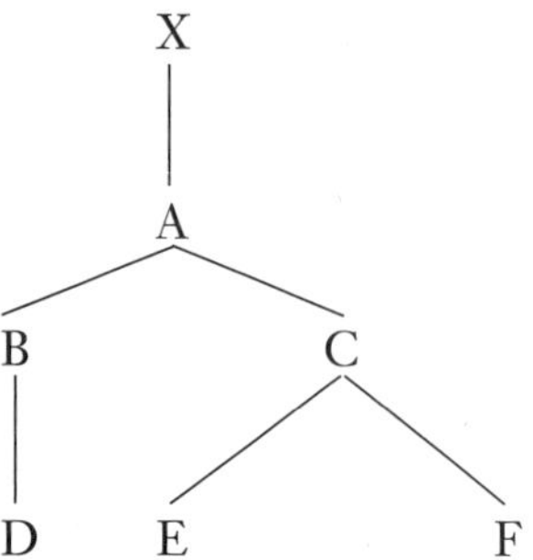

On the other hand, if A dies childless *before* division, he simply disappears. The remaining two brothers will eventually divide their father's estate as if their dead brother had never existed. The land that A shared in his lifetime will have a title deed like this:

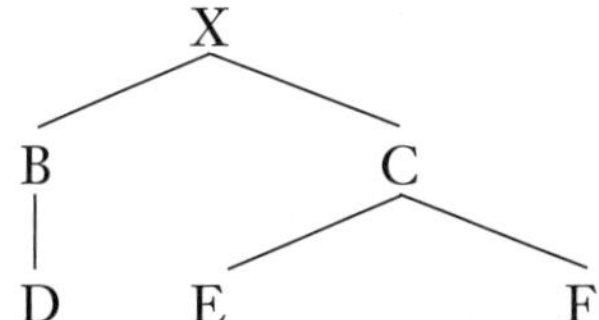

For reasons connected apparently with the afterlife, it was thought necessary that A should have a stake in the family land in this world (Brichto 1973). In that way his "name" would be preserved. The levirate marriage, between A's widow and one of his surviving brothers, provides A with a fictional son who will take his "father's" share alongside the shares of his uncles.

Disputes between undivided brothers are adumbrated in Isaac's blessing in Genesis 27:29. Isaac blesses Jacob in the mistaken belief that it is his firstborn Esau: "Be master over your brothers and let your mother's sons bow down to you." While there are political overtones to his declaration, the model seems to be the legal one of a father deciding who is to continue as head of household after his death. As in Egypt, Isaac assigns the privilege of managing the joint estate, he thinks, to his firstborn.

The next stage is division of the estate by the heirs, for which the Bible provides evidence in an unexpected source. While ownership of the promised land was based on a divine grant, it has been pointed out that the actual allocation of land among the tribes when they at last enter Canaan follows the standard procedure for division of inheritance known from cuneiform law codes and legal documents (Kitz 2000). The land is first divided into parcels, and the parcels are then allocated by the casting of lots (Josh. 13:6–7; 14:1–2; 17:3–6; 18:1–11). It is a logical step, since the twelve tribes of Israel are in effect inheriting the estate of their father Jacob.

All the heirs receive equal shares, except for the firstborn, who, in accord with the prevailing custom in the neighboring countries, receives a double share (Deut. 21:17). This extra share could be sold as a future interest, as we learn from an incident involving Esau. Returning from the hunt famished, he is persuaded to sell his firstborn right (usually translated "birthright") to Jacob for a bowl of lentil soup (Gen. 25:27–34).

B. Line of Succession

Since all the sons belonging to the "house of the father" inherit together, there is no need to rank them as heirs. If there are no sons, then the law must decide which of more distant relatives has priority in inheriting.

In the ancient world, the general principle was that, failing heirs within the patriarchal household, the estate passed to the members of the extended family or clan. The Gortyn Code sets out the sequence of succession in detail (V 9–28):

> When a man or woman dies, if there be children or children's children or children's children's children, they shall have the property. And if there be none of these, but brothers of the deceased and brother's children or brother's children's children, they shall have the property. And if there be none of these, those to whom the property may fall as kinsmen shall take it up. And if there be no kinsmen, then those of the household who constitute the estate shall have the property.

The Bible sets out a clear line of intestate succession that follows the same principles (Num. 27:8–11):

> If a man dies and has no son, you shall transfer his landed estate to his daughter. And if he has no daughter, you shall give his landed inheritance to his brothers. And if he has no brothers, you shall give his landed inheritance to his father's brothers. And if his father has no brothers, you shall give his landed inheritance to his kinsman who is closest to him in his clan, and he shall inherit it.

After the "house of the father" is exhausted, the law ensures that family property at least stays within the clan. Daughters do not automatically inherit as legitimate heirs but are legitimate enough to inherit by default in the absence of sons. This passage gives them precedence over more distant male relatives, but as we shall see below, the rule is subject to conditions.

One biblical narrative hints at other possibilities for inheritance in the absence of sons. In the genealogical lists of Chronicles, we are told that a certain Sheshan had no sons; so he gave his daughter in marriage to his Egyptian slave, Jarha (1 Chr. 2:34–35). As the purpose must have been to provide Sheshan with a direct heir (and a legitimate grandson), it is probable that the slave was freed at the same time, and possibly even adopted by his father-in-law.

According to Genesis 15:2–3, a childless Abram's successor will be his servant Eliezer. The Hebrew term (*ben-mešek*) is obscure and may refer to a steward or a house-born slave. There is nothing in Near Eastern sources that would allow for such a solution, but it is essentially the same as we have just seen in the Gortyn Code. Of course, Abram still had a living relative, his nephew Lot, who seems to have been forgotten, even though Abram and Lot had at one time held their property in common like undivided heirs (using the technical term "dwell together" in Gen. 13:5–6).

C. Female Succession

The primary way in which a woman acquires property is by dowry. The dowry is a portion of her own family's assets that her father gives her upon marriage.

It may be supplemented with gifts from other sources, such as the groom or his family.

The dowry accompanies the bride into her husband's household. There it is subsumed into her husband's assets but continues to exist in theory as a fund that she may reclaim during widowhood and that will ultimately be inherited by her children. In most systems a small part of the dowry constitutes a trousseau—personal property that does remain under the wife's control. In rabbinic law it is referred to as *melog* property, a term that is also found in Ugaritic and Akkadian. In Greek, it is called *phernē*.

These are the main lines of an institution—the dowry—that is virtually universal in the ancient world. It must have been equally central to the law of biblical Israel, although one would hardly imagine it from its appearance in the Bible. Biblical Hebrew has a technical term for dowry, *šilluḥim*, but it is exceedingly rare (1 Kgs. 9:16; Mic. 1:14). Otherwise, the few overt references to dowry are so elliptical that they have seldom been recognized as such. Nonetheless, dowry plays an important role behind the scenes in various biblical laws and narratives.

The dowry is sometimes recognizable from its content. Laban gives a personal maid to each of his daughters on her wedding (Gen. 29:24, 29). In Ezekiel 16:10–12, God as groom gives clothes and jewelry to his bride, Israel, who as an orphan can expect nothing from her own family. Likewise, in the case of Rebecca, we are not told expressly of any gifts from her father, but she does receive presents of silver, gold, and clothing from Abraham's servant and, when setting out with him, is accompanied by her personal maids (Gen. 24:53, 61). Finally, Proverbs 31:10–31 tells us that a capable wife has a worth far above rubies and lists her virtues in terms of economy and commerce. Rubies are not a medium of exchange but are the sort of property that was most likely to be found in a dowry. The message is that a hardworking wife with a good head for business is more profitable to her husband in the long run than one who comes with a rich dowry.

In the above cases, the maids remain under the control of the wife and may thus be regarded as a trousseau. Rachel and Leah certainly retain control of their maids, for they are later both in a position to give their maids to Jacob in order to bear children (Gen. 30:3–4, 9). Likewise, Sarai's maid Hagar, whom she gives to Abram, must have been part of her trousseau (Gen. 16:2–3). In Ezekiel's metaphor, Israel as wife abuses her control over all her husband's gifts of clothing and jewelry (Ezek. 16:16–18).

Including land in the dowry raises practical problems, because the bride can hardly take it with her to the house of a distant groom. Nonetheless, the Bible gives several instances of land as dowry. The proximity problem is elegantly resolved by the Pharaoh when he gives his daughter in marriage to

King Solomon: in order to provide a suitable dowry, he sacks the Canaanite city of Gezer, which lay on the border between the two kingdoms (1 Kgs. 9:16). Achsah persuades her father Caleb to add land with springs to her dowry so that they may irrigate her husband's land (Josh. 15:18–19; Judg. 1:13–15). When his fortunes were restored, Job was so wealthy that he could afford to give his daughters estates of land (*nahalah*; Job 42:15).

Two factors distinguish dowry from inheritance: it is given during the lifetime of the father, and it is legally speaking a voluntary gift, whereas inheritance is a vested future right. It is for these reasons that the daughter is only a secondary heir, in the event that there are no male heirs. She already has received her share of the family assets upon marriage, and even if she has not, she has only a moral, not a legal claim to a share.

Although western Asiatic societies privilege the male heir, a few do impose an automatic rule of succession that, in the absence of male heirs, the daughters are to inherit. Some societies find other solutions, however, in particular special dispositions by a testator (see below). The documentary record hints at an ongoing struggle between the deceased's residual male heirs (brothers or uncles) and his daughters, which the courts resolved sometimes in favor of the former and sometimes in favor of the latter (Paradise 1987).

Even when the daughter becomes an heiress in her own right, the dowry model still reflects the attitude of the law. Already the Sumerian law code of Lipit-Ishtar provides (LL b):

> If a man dies and has no son, his unmarried daughter shall be his heir.

The reason for insisting that the daughter be unmarried is that a married daughter will already have received her dowry. The inheritance share is therefore conceived of as a form of dowry. This conception raises problems, because a dowry is in effect a transfer of ancestral property from the daughter's family to her husband's family.

The Gortyn Code recognizes a daughter's right to inherit alongside her brothers but places restrictions on her when in the absence of brothers she is the sole heiress. Its approach is as follows (VII 15–24):

> The heiress is to be married to the brother of her father, the oldest of those living. And if there be more heiresses and brothers of the father, they are to be married to the next oldest. And if there should be no brothers of the father, but sons of the brothers, she is to be married to that one (who is the son) of the oldest.

The ruling is a compromise between the rights of the deceased's daughters and the rights of his male heirs in the clan who would be next in line to inherit if the house of the father were to be deemed extinct. The identical approach is adopted in the Bible in the case of the daughters of Zelophehad.

The case is presented as an original problem that arose prior to occupation of the promised land (Num. 27:1–11). Zelophehad died leaving five daughters and no sons. On the assumption that only sons inherited, the daughters complained to Moses, who referred their case to God. The ruling, as we have seen, is presented as a precedent: in the absence of sons, daughters are next in line to inherit, taking precedence over the deceased's male kinsmen. In a postscript to the story, however, the deceased's brothers in turn complain to Moses. As a result, the daughters are obliged to marry the next male heirs in line, namely, their cousins, so that the land, regarded as dowry, should not be lost to the clan (Num. 36:1–12).

One person who is missing from the list of heirs is the wife. She must look to her dowry for her support after her husband's death. Some Near Eastern law codes provide for the widow to receive a share of her late husband's estate, at least for her lifetime. The biblical codes are not among them, although it has been suggested that one of the secondary purposes of the levirate is to provide support for the widow, through remarriage (Thompson 1968). In biblical Israel, if the widow had no dowry or other means of support, then she would join the Levite, the orphan, and the alien as deprived, landless members of society who are entitled to humanitarian aid (Deut. 14:28–29).

D. Testamentary Powers

The ancient world had the concept of a last will and testament, but not in the modern sense. A father's power to make a will was severely restricted, especially as regards capital assets such as land. Because his sons had vested rights to equal inheritance shares, a father could not simply disinherit one son or give family property to an outsider. He did, however, have limited powers to dispose of assets within the circle of potential heirs. He could assign certain property to one share or another, rearrange the shares among the heirs, especially by transferring the firstborn's share to a younger son, and include daughters and wives among the heirs. What he could not do in principle was to give away property to persons beyond the members of the patriarchal household.

Testaments exploiting these limited powers are well represented among ancient Near Eastern legal documents, with arrangements of remarkable complexity. The following example is from fifteenth-century Nuzi (Annual of the American Schools of Oriental Research X, no. 21):

> Tablet of allocation of Ziki son of Akkuya: he has fixed the allocations of his sons Ellu and Arziza. Thus Ziki declares:

"As regards all my fields, Ellu is my eldest son, and he shall take a double inheritance-share; Arzizza is the younger son and he shall take according to his share."

Thus Ziki declares: "I have given my houses and fields in Nuzi to my eldest son, Ellu.

"I have given my stable which is among the large buildings together with its vehicles, to Arzizza, and Arzizza may open its entrance to the street. I have given my storehouses[?] in upper Nuzi beside the storehouses[?] of A. to Arzizza."

Thus Ziki declares: "My son Shennima has taken the fields, houses, and all the property of my brother Shurihil; therefore Shennima shall not be included as heir to the fields, houses, and property of my father Akkuya. He shall not divide their property with Ellu and Arzizza.

"Ellu and Arzizza shall divide my storehouses[?] in upper Nuzi beside the storehouses[?] of B. Ellu shall take a double portion and Arzizza shall take according to his share.

"Of the slave-girls, each one shall take according to his share."

Thus Ziki declares: "If Shennima presses claims against Ellu and Arzizza concerning my fields, houses, and property, Shennima shall pay Ellu and Arzizza two mina of silver and two mina of gold."

Thus Ziki declares: "On this day I have made a disposition and this tablet is a tablet; any other tablet is no tablet."

And thus Ziki declares: "Whichever of my sons sells a field or a house shall forfeit his fields and houses."

(nine witnesses and scribe)

This tablet was written after proclamation in Nuzi at the city gate.

A testament was the prime means of transferring property to wives and daughters. A husband could make a gift to his wife that could theoretically disenfranchise his sons, although most such bequests were designed only to support her during widowhood, the property then reverting to the primary heirs. In order to strengthen the widow's position against other heirs, the testator could also assign a different status to her. Thus testaments from Nuzi and Emar give the widow the status of "father" or of "father and mother." An Egyptian testator adopts his widow as his daughter (Gardiner 1941):

Year one, third month of summer, day twenty, under the majesty of the King of Upper and Lower Egypt, Ramses.

On this day, proclamation to [the god] Amun of the accession of this noble god, he arising and shining forth, and making offering to Amun. Thereupon Nebnefer, my husband, made a writing for me, Nanefer, the musician of [the god] Seth, and made me a daughter of his, and wrote down for me all that he possessed, having no son or daughter apart from myself:

"All profit that I have made with her, I will bequeath it to Nanefer, my wife, and if any of my own brothers or sisters arise to confront her

> at my death tomorrow or thereafter and say: 'Let my brother's share be given [to me] . . .'"
>
> Before many and numerous witnesses: [names] "Behold, I have made the bequest to Nanefer, my wife, this day before Huyyeremw, my sister."

Similar precautions are adopted by testators for their daughters, whom they sometimes adopt as sons in order to protect them better from the claims of other heirs, although it was not strictly necessary.

Some of these powers are documented in the Bible, where a father contemplating death is said to "give orders regarding his house" (2 Sam. 17:23; 2 Kgs. 20:1; Isa. 38:1). To begin with, the father could shift the firstborn's extra share from his biologically eldest son to a younger son. Deuteronomy 21:15–17 recognizes this right while placing limitations on it. The text envisions a situation where the father has two sons from two different wives, where the one wife is "loved" and the other "hated," and where the eldest is the son of the "hated" wife. In this situation, the father could not deprive the firstborn son of the extra share in favor of the younger. The text seems to confirm that fathers could, in general, grant the status of firstborn to a younger son, but it forbids such action in this specific situation. The question then becomes how to understand this situation and, more particularly, how to understand the terms "loved" and "hated." Most scholars assume that the terms refer to a general preference that the husband has for one of his wives and not for the other. Others have suggested more specific meanings: "hated" means "divorced" (Rabinowicz 1953), or "hated" means demoted from first-ranking wife, and "loved" means promoted to first-ranking wife (Szubin and Porten 2001).

The political history of the settlement in the promised land at times represents the preeminence of the two tribes of Ephraim and Manasseh in terms of inheritance. As the sons of Joseph, they should theoretically have been entitled to only a half-share each, and yet they each receive a full share. The explanation in Joshua is purely pragmatic: being numerous, they require more land (Josh. 17:14–18). The explanation in Chronicles, however, is that Jacob transferred to Joseph the firstborn Reuben's extra share because Reuben had slept with his father's concubine (1 Chr. 5:1). Reuben's offense is recorded in Genesis 35:22, and in the so-called "Blessing of Jacob" he is stripped of his firstborn status for the same reason (Gen. 49:3–4). In Genesis 48:21, a slightly different version is offered: the dying Jacob gives Joseph an extra gift as his favorite son. Taking all these sources into consideration, the situation seems to have been that a father could transfer the extra share to a favorite son, but would not normally deprive his firstborn of the privilege without cause.

A father could designate his daughters as heirs with equal rights to their brothers, as Job did, although it may have been intended as dowry, since he continued to live long after the gift (Job 42:15). As a husband, he could give his wife a bequest, as is hinted at in Jeremiah 3:19. The verse also suggests that the husband adopted his wife as a daughter, a legal maneuver known from the Egyptian Adoption Papyrus.

Finally, a father could remember his illegitimate sons. Abraham gave his sons by his concubines gifts, not land, in his lifetime and sent them away (Gen. 25:5–6).

Further Reading

Some titles have been abbreviated; see bibliography for full citations.

Ben-Barak, Z. 1981. "Meribaal and the System of Land Grants," 73–91.

———. 2006. *Inheritance by Daughters*, 13–108.

Berlin, A. 1987. "On the Interpretation of Psalm 133," 141–47.

Brichto, H. C. 1973. "Kin, Cult, Land and Afterlife," 1–32.

Brin, G. 1994. "The Laws of Inheritance of the First-Born," in *Studies in Biblical Law*, 238–63.

Daube, D. 1950. "Consortium in Roman and Hebrew Law," 71–77, 89–91.

Dearman, J. A. 1988. *Property Rights in the Eighth-Century Prophets*, 108–27.

Fleishman, J. 2007. "'Their Father Gave Them *nahala* "an estate,"'" 120–34.

Gardiner, A. H. 1941. "Adoption Extraordinary," 23–29.

Kitz, A. M. 2000. "Undivided Inheritance and Lot Casting in the Book of Joshua," 601–18.

Machinist, P. 1998. "Job's Daughters and Their Inheritance," 71–72.

Paradise, J. S. 1987. "Daughters as 'Sons' at Nuzi," 203–13.

Szubin, H. Z., and B. Porten. 2001. "The Status of a Repudiated Spouse," 46–78.

Thompson, T., and D. Thompson. 1968. "Some Legal Problems in the Book of Ruth," 79–99.

Westbrook, R. 1991. *Property and the Family*: chap. 4: The Law of the Biblical Levirate, 69–89; chap. 6: Undivided Inheritance, 118–41; chap. 7: The Dowry, 142–64.

Questions for Review

1. What is a "royal land grant," and what is probably the best example of such a grant in the Bible?
2. In the Priestly source, the Levites are the recipients of the people's tithes. They, in turn, are supposed to offer a tithe from what they receive. Who is the recipient of their tithe?
   a. Moses
   b. priests
   c. widows and orphans
   d. non-Israelites who are part of the Israelite community

3. Throughout the ancient Near East, daughters often did not count as legitimate heirs of their father's estate. What, then, did daughters typically receive instead of receiving a normal inheritance share?
   a. gifts from their mother
   b. the betrothal payment that their husband-to-be paid to their family
   c. a dowry that they took with them when they were married
   d. nothing; all the family property went to the sons
4. What was the most common privilege that fell to firstborn sons when it came time for them to receive their inheritance?
   a. an extra inheritance share; they received two, all other sons only one
   b. the right to administer how their father's estate would be divided
   c. the right to select which property and goods would be part of their inheritance share
   d. the right to take their inheritance share and establish their own household prior to their father's death
5. The so-called custom of the levirate is referred to in the Bible several times. In each instance, though, it is put into practice only under which particular condition?
   a. The man who died childless had already received his inheritance share.
   b. The man who died childless had no surviving brothers.
   c. The man who died childless was living as part of an undivided estate.
   d. The man who died childless had been promoted to firstborn status by his father, even though he was not the biologically oldest son.
6. According to the Bible, who stands to inherit a man's estate (i.e., what is the order of succession) if he dies childless?
   a. the man's brothers, then the cousins on his father's side
   b. the man's brothers, then his paternal uncles
   c. the man's brothers, then his nephews
   d. the man's brothers, then his wife's brothers
7. According to two passages in Numbers, under what conditions may daughters inherit their father's property when he dies with no surviving sons?
   a. if they agree to marry their cousins
   b. if they agree never to sell the property
   c. if they agree never to marry
   d. if they agree to care for their mother until her death
8. What is the purpose for the condition that is identified in question 7 above?
9. According to a passage in Deuteronomy, under what conditions may a father not promote a younger son to the status of firstborn?
10. What is the term for the mechanism (usually recorded in a document) that was a man's primary means for transferring property to his wife or to his daughter(s)?
    a. contract
    b. deposition
    c. precedent
    d. testament

Answers

1. A royal land grant occurs when a king gives a tract or several tracts of land to one or more of his citizens. In the Bible, several texts use the model of the royal land grant to describe the giving of the promised land by God to the Israelites.
2. The answer is (b). Every priest was a Levite (that is, believed to have descended from Jacob's son, Levi), but not every Levite was a priest. Thus the idea was for the people to support the Levites and for the latter to support those special few who had been chosen to function as the people's representatives before God.
3. The answer is (c). Without a dowry from her family, it was unlikely that a young woman would obtain a husband. The larger and more luxurious the dowry, the better her chances of attracting well-to-do suitors.
4. The answer is (a). This was particularly true of the societies in western Asia and is explicitly referred to in Deuteronomy 21:15–17.
5. The answer is (c). As far as we can tell, the practice of levirate marriage takes place only when the man who died was living within an undivided estate. Such an estate is one where the brothers have not yet divided their father's estate and taken their individual inheritance shares. An estate could be undivided because the brothers' father, the head of household, is still alive or because, even after the father's death, there may have been reasons to keep the estate intact temporarily.
6. The answer is (b). The line of succession given in Numbers 27:8–11, for a man who dies childless, begins with the man's brothers, then moves to his paternal uncles, and then goes to the next closest male relative on his father's side.

7–8. Daughters can inherit their father's property only if they agree to marry their cousins (a). The Bible reports this as the result of negotiations between Zelophehad's daughters, Zelophehad's brothers, and Moses (who consults God). The brothers are concerned about seeing these daughters marry outside the clan (or extended family) and thereby seeing Zelophehad's land disappear into the holdings of another clan. Daughters in this situation had to marry within the extended family in order to keep the land within that family.

9. He may not do so when he has a "loved" wife and a "hated" wife, and when the oldest son is the son of the "hated" wife. Exactly what the terms "loved" and "hated" mean in this context is not entirely clear. See the paragraph on Deuteronomy 21:15–17 on page 103.
10. The answer is (d). One could think of it as a "last will and testament," though there are significant differences between the ancient and modern versions.

6

Contracts

> Contracts, both explicit and implied, infuse our everyday lives. Whether in the grocery store, at the marriage altar, or in the workplace, many of our daily activities are governed by contractual rules. This was also true to a large degree in biblical Israel and throughout the ancient Near East. This chapter presents a variety of contracts used in biblical Israel that help us to understand how business was conducted in the ancient world. It also looks at the issue of social justice and related rules from the Bible that appear to be much more in the nature of utopian ideals rather than actual facets of everyday law.

A contract is a private agreement that is enforceable in law. It is also an agreement into which the two parties enter, at least in theory, voluntarily. Records of contracts are by far the most common type of document preserved in ancient Near Eastern sources, running into the tens of thousands. They give us a valuable insight into everyday legal practice among Israel's neighbors. The legal theory behind these arrangements is more difficult to recover. The contracts themselves assume the law and do nothing to explain it, while the casuistic paragraphs of the law codes resolve practical issues relating to specific contracts without going into the general principles underpinning contractual liability. Nonetheless, it is possible to discern from the sources two ways in which contractual obligation could arise: by "real" contract and by promissory oath.

A *real contract* is an agreement involving mutual obligations where one party has already performed his side of the bargain. That performance is the basis for being able to claim performance by the other party. Although it could apply in theory to any partly performed agreement, we find that the recorded real contracts tend to be standard transactions such as sale, hire, loan, and partnership. There was an obvious convenience in following the pattern of a conventional arrangement, since the parties would not need to spell out all the terms of the contract. They could be implied from customary usage.

A *promissory oath* is a solemn self-curse. The promissor invites a deity or the king to punish him, should he fail to fulfill the terms of the promise. It takes the form of a solemn declaration along the lines: "May the god X do such and such to me (e.g., kill or visit with sickness) if I do not do Y." When the promise is to the benefit of another person, the oath may be regarded as a form of contract.

The oath created a unilateral obligation, although it could be made bilateral by reciprocal oaths. It was a very flexible instrument that could be applied to add terms to a standard contract or to create an independent contract. Evidently it was an oral procedure, but the same is true of the real contract. Although they are preserved only in written form, the essence of a contract was an oral agreement before witnesses, which occasionally would be written down for the sake of supplementing the witnesses' memories.

Ancient Israel lacks archival records and the Hebrew Bible has little interest in everyday contracts. While the Mishpatim regulate a few commercial contracts, the primary interest of the biblical law codes, as indeed of the prophets, in the law of contracts is in measures of social justice to temper their harsh application to the poor and weaker members of society (see below). Biblical narratives do occasionally recount the formation and use of contracts, sometimes of a standard form and sometimes to emphasize the unusual and indeed bizarre character of the arrangement. Enough of the principles of contract law emerge even from such cases to give us an idea of how contracts worked in everyday life.

The Hebrew term for contract is *briyt*, which is used for private contracts, international treaties, and pacts between Israel and God (often translated "covenant"). Most contracts are not, however, explicitly designated as such. From the biblical accounts, the same two basic types of contractual obligation can be discerned, as in the rest of the ancient Near East: real contracts and promissory oaths.

1. REAL CONTRACTS

There is evidence for the following standard real contracts: sale, hire, deposit, loan (and ancillary contracts ensuring security for the debt), agency, betrothal, and partnership.

A. Sale

A number of narratives report the purchase of land, two of them in great detail. In Genesis 23, Abraham purchases the cave of Machpelah from Ephron the Hittite after complex negotiations. The complication is that Abraham is a foreign resident and must therefore have the approval of the local government to purchase land from a local citizen. When the transaction is completed, the property of the seller is said to pass to Abraham both in the presence of the Hittites (Gen. 23:17–18) and from the Hittites, as if they were the seller (v. 20). This reflects a method of confirming sales found at Ugarit in the thirteenth century (no. 15.119 in Nougayrol 1955):

> From this day, before Niqmepa son of Niqmadu, king of Ugarit, Yaheshar son of Mashu has acquired the house of Hagbanu son of Ili-shala for x sheqels of silver. The house is bound in the sun of the day to Yaheshar and his sons forever.
>
> In the first place, Hagbanu has given it, and in the second place, Niqmepa son of Niqmadu, king of Ugarit, has given it to Yaheshar and to his sons forever.

Formal similarities have also been noted with Neo-Babylonian dialogue documents (eighth to sixth century), where a summary account of the negotiations is given as part of the record. For example, the sale of a house is recorded as follows (no. 26 in San Nicolò 1951):

> Iba son of Balatsu went to Remutu son of Dummuqu and said: "I will give you my house, and please give me the silver, so that I may pay my creditors." Remutu son of Dummuqu heard him, and he weighed out and gave him eighty-three shekels of silver. He (Iba) then transferred to him the constructed house, the built-in door jamb, and the door with bolt fastened.
>
> Upper side: the Avenue; lower side: Bel-iddin son of Apla; upper front: Narrow Street; lower front: Amel-Shamash.
>
> [The silver] is given; he [Iba] has received it; he is paid, quit.
>
> . . .
>
> (five witnesses)

The possibility of influences from as far apart as the thirteenth and the sixth centuries suggests caution in dating the law in biblical narratives. Both the law and the story may considerably antedate the final version found in the biblical text.

The account of Jeremiah's purchase of his nephew Hanamael's land at Anathoth gives further details of the ceremony, especially the summoning of witnesses and the weighing of the silver for the purchase price (Jer. 32:6–15).

It emphasizes the recording of the transaction in writing, referring to the sealed and open documents of purchase. This practice has been discussed previously, in chapter 2, on litigation (pp. 43–44).

A feature that these two narratives share with the other accounts of purchase of land (Gen. 33:18–20; 2 Sam. 24:24; 1 Kgs. 16:24) is the express mention of the purchase price in weight of silver. The same is true of the many thousands of land-sale documents from the ancient Near East. Behind this mention lies a fundamental principle of the law of sale: full payment of the purchase price was necessary to transfer ownership in land. The biblical narratives therefore emphasize that the purchasers—Abraham, Jacob, King David, King Omri, and Jeremiah—had all acquired full ownership in the land by legitimate, completed purchase.

Moreover, a second principle may have been at stake. As between private individuals, a gift of family land was valid only for the lifetime of the donor; it could not override the vested rights of the donor's heirs, who would repossess the land when it came time to claim their inheritance. To acquire a permanent estate, the buyer must pay the full market price. As a contract from Susa puts it (no. 44 in Scheil 1930):

> Not redemption, not pledge; full price. As a father buys for his son, Ninshubur-abi has bought [this house] under the protection of [the god] Shushinak for ever [lit. for generations].

It is for this reason that Abraham insists on paying the full price when the landowner, Ephron, proposes to give him the land. Likewise, King David insists on paying Araunah, an inhabitant of the city that he has just conquered, the full price for his threshing floor.

B. Hire

The hire of persons is frequently mentioned in the Bible, but the legal conditions of the contract hardly at all. Wages, which appear to be entirely a matter of free bargaining, could be paid in silver (Zech. 11:12) or goods (Gen. 38:16–17) and could be determined on the basis of the hireling's time or the specific service performed. The clearest example of a time-based hire is the day laborer, who is economically and socially among the lowest orders, scarcely better off than a slave (Lev. 25:6; Job 7:1–2; Hag. 1:6). So needy is he and open to exploitation (Mal. 3:5) that it is forbidden to delay payment of his wages until the following day, although only a divine sanction is prescribed (Lev. 19:13; Deut. 24:14–15).

Longer terms of hire were also known, customarily year by year (Lev. 25:50, 53; Isa. 21:16) or a three-year term (Deut. 15:18; Isa. 21:16). The seven-year contracts that Laban made with Jacob may have been pointedly excessive (Gen. 29:15; 30:28–33; 31:7–8; see below).

The services that could be engaged through a contract of hire were unlimited in scope, including disreputable as well as honest professions. Reputable services were, for example, those of a craftsman (Isa. 46:6; 2 Chr. 24:12), a priest (Judg. 17:7–12; 18:4), or a wet nurse (Exod. 2:9). The hire of a wet nurse is recorded in Mesopotamia, where it could be a three-year term. According to LE 32,

> If a man gives his son for wet-nursing and rearing but does not give grain, oil, and wool for three years, he shall pay 10 shekels of silver for his son's rearing and may fetch his son.

Less reputable but perfectly valid were the hire of a prophet to curse one's enemy (Num. 22–24; Deut. 23:4; Neh. 13:2), of mercenaries for a military campaign (2 Sam. 10:6; Isa. 7:20; 1 Chr. 19:6–7), and of a prostitute (Gen. 38:12–18; Deut. 23:18; Mic. 1:7). The hire of assassins (Judg. 9:4) and the bribing of courtiers (Ezra 4:5), although referred to in the same terms, would undoubtedly not have been regarded as valid contracts by a contemporary court. A good example of a bizarre contract in the narratives, perhaps meant sarcastically, is Leah's remark to her husband Jacob that she has hired his sexual services for the night from Rachel for the price of some mandrakes (Gen. 30:16–18).

A specialized contract with close Near Eastern parallels is the herding contract. It is the only commercial contract to be regulated in detail in the law codes, and its application is also recorded in the patriarchal narratives in Genesis. Exodus 22:9–12 presents it as a simple deposit with one's neighbor, but Mesopotamian parallels show that it is a standard contract whereby a shepherd is hired to look after a person's animals (as in no. 16.224 in Szlechter 1958):

> twelve rams, five ewes, three lambs; total, twenty animals that Ilshu-ibnishu entrusted to Ilshu-bani for herding. He [Ilshu-bani] is liable for mangled or lost animals. (Scribe as witness)

The biblical law provides that the shepherd has to replace animals from the herd that are stolen, but not those that die of natural causes or are taken by force majeure or by wild animals. Similarly, CH 266 provides,

> If disease should break out or a lion should kill in the sheepfold, the shepherd shall take an exculpatory oath before the god, and the owner of the sheepfold shall absorb the losses suffered in the sheepfold.

The detailed sources from Mesopotamia reveal that contracts tended to be annual and that the animals were to be delivered to the owner at shearing time. The shepherd could be remunerated in a variety of ways, ranging from an advanced payment to a share in the herd's increase above a certain minimum reserved for the owner. The same type of contract is agreed upon by Laban and Jacob, but for terms of seven years and for more exotic wages: Jacob is to receive the hand of Laban's daughters in marriage and the speckled and spotted sheep and goats (Gen. 29:15–20, 25–27; 30:28–34), although Laban apparently unilaterally altered these terms (Gen. 31:41).

The hire of animals is mentioned only incidentally in a law relating to the death or injury of borrowed animals (Exod. 22:14).

C. Deposit

A contract of deposit is an arrangement whereby the owner of property entrusts it to another for safekeeping. The depositee may be remunerated for his trouble, but this is not an essential element of the contract, as is the price for sale or the wage for hire. It is regulated in the Mishpatim as regards the liability of the depositee if the property is stolen, but unfortunately the provision is enigmatic and has been interpreted in many different ways (Exod. 22:6–8). It would appear that the depositee was liable for his own dishonest misappropriation, but it is not clear if he would be liable for negligence. At all events, the required standard of care is lower than that of the shepherd, who receives remuneration for looking after another's property.

The narratives again contain some extraordinary types of deposit. In the Joseph story in Genesis, Reuben offers Jacob a contract of deposit: Jacob is to place Benjamin in his safekeeping for a journey. The sanction that Reuben proposes for failing to meet his contractual obligation (i.e., not bringing Benjamin back safely) is vicarious liability: the right of Jacob to kill Reuben's own two sons (Gen. 42:37). Jacob does not accept the offer but does agree to a later proposal by Judah that he himself be liable for Benjamin's safety (Gen. 43:8–10). Unfortunately, the exact penalty that he proposes is unclear and is usually translated by bland phrases such as "I shall stand guilty before you forever" (JPS).

In 1 Kings 20:39–40, a soldier agrees to guard a prisoner of war on the following terms: "if he goes missing, it is your life for his, or you shall pay a talent of silver." The penalty for breach of contract is therefore death, unless the guard can ransom his life with an impossibly high sum. The king, to whom the soldier appeals after losing his prisoner, can see nothing wrong with the contract.

D. Loan

The many thousands of loan contracts from the ancient Near East record a wide range of loans, from commercial to consumer, with a rich variety of terms, regarding interest, repayment, and security in case the debtor fails to repay the loan.

The two universal forms of security were pledge and suretyship (guarantor). Pledge could be of any asset belonging to the debtor—land, movables, or persons—and could include members of the debtor's family and even the debtor himself. Pledges could be hypothecary or possessory. With a *hypothecary pledge*, the property remained with the debtor and was seized by the creditor only in the event of default. An example of a loan secured by a hypothecary pledge comes from Elephantine (no. B3.1 in Porten and Yardeni 1989 = no. 10 in Cowley 1923):

> On the seventh of Kislev, which is the fourth day of the month Thoth, year nine of Artaxerxes the king, Yehohen daughter of Meshullakh, a woman of Fort Elephantine, declared to Meshullam son of Zakkur, a Jew of Fort Elephantine:
>
> "You have given me a loan of silver, four shekels by the royal weight, at a rate of interest that will accrue against me of two hallur of silver per shekel per month, namely eight hallur of silver per month. If the interest turns into capital, the interest shall accrue [interest] like capital, one like the other.
>
> "And if a second year arrives and I have not paid you your capital and the interest thereon that is written in this deed, you Meshullam and your sons are entitled to take for yourself any pledge that you find belonging to me—a brick-built house, silver and gold, copper and iron, male and female slave, barley, emmer, and any foodstuff that you find belonging to me until you have satisfied your [claim of] silver and its interest.
>
> "And I will not be able to say to you, 'I have paid you your silver and its interest' as long as this deed is in your possession, nor will I be able to raise a plea against you before a commander or judge to say, 'You took a pledge from me' as long as this deed is in your possession.
>
> "And if I die and I have not paid you this silver and its interest, my sons shall pay you this silver and its interest, and if they do not pay you this silver and its interest, you Meshullam are entitled to take for yourself any foodstuffs and pledge that you find belonging to them until you have satisfied your [claim of] silver and its interest.
>
> "And they will not be able to raise a plea against you before a commander or judge as long as this deed is in your possession. Moreover, if they do litigate, they shall not prevail as long as this deed is in your possession."
>
> (Scribe, four witnesses)

A *possessory pledge* was taken by the creditor at the outset of the loan and could be used or exploited by the creditor pending repayment. Where land or persons were the security, a common form was antichretic pledge: the creditor enjoyed the income from the land or from the person's labor in lieu of interest payments. It should be emphasized that this was still a contractual arrangement: neither the land nor the person so pledged became the property of the creditor, unless the debtor defaulted when the debt fell due. An example from Emar from the fourteenth century reads (text A in Tsukimoto 1988):

> Dudu son of Mashru together with his sons Kiri-Dagan and Abdi-ili were resident as antichretic pledges of She'i-Dagan for 105 shekels forty grains of silver. Now Dudu has repaid forty shekels of that silver and has released himself. Kiri-Dagan and Abdi-ili remain resident in the house of She'i-Dagan for sixty-five shekels forty grains of silver.
>
> . . .
>
> While he was resident in the house of She'i-Dagan, Dudu was released for nine months and went away. When Dudu repays the silver in full, he shall give She'i-Dagan one son and he shall do service for nine months. (six witnesses)

In case of default, a creditor could seize property or family members of the debtor and hold them in order to force the debtor to pay up. But the creditor could not exploit them as he could with a pledge and, in the absence of a contractual pledge, it would appear that the creditor could not simply acquire ownership of the debtor's property or enslave the debtor or his family. Nonetheless, the pressure that a creditor could bring to bear would often force the debtor to sell his land, family, or himself into slavery when he was unable to repay the debt.

Nehemiah 5:3–5 neatly illustrates these principles of law and practice concerning debt and security:

> Others said, "We must pledge our fields, our vineyards, and our homes to get grain to stave off hunger." Yet others said, "We have borrowed silver against our fields and vineyards to pay the king's tax. Now we are as good as our brothers, and our children as good as theirs; yet here we are subjecting our sons and daughters to slavery—some of our daughters are already subjected—and we are powerless, while our fields and vineyards belong to others."

We learn from verse 11 that the loans were in silver, grain, wine, and oil. Evidently, the silver was used to pay the taxes mentioned in the above passage, and the foodstuffs were famine loans. Security for the famine loans was the debtors' homes and agricultural land, while for the silver loans it was only the agricultural land. The latter appears already to have been seized for default. Lacking security for further credit, the debtors are now obliged to hand over their children as debt-slaves. The foodstuffs lent are durable in nature and therefore could serve as currency like silver. Repayment would not necessarily be in the same currency. Food loans are also attested in Leviticus 25:35–37 and Deuteronomy 23:20, and Leviticus 25:37 makes clear that interest was chargeable on a food loan.

The Bible is not very informative on the question of interest. The Torah's few provisions are prohibitions on interest, which led to the complete ban on usury (which originally meant charging any interest) in some Christian teachings. Whether the ban in the Torah was as comprehensive as that, or even actionable in a human court, is less certain. The moneylender was regarded with contempt (Ps. 15:5; Prov. 28:8), and Ezekiel threatens him with divine punishment. At the same time, however, he was regarded as a part of the social order and could even be an instrument of divine punishment (Ps. 109:11–12). Exodus 22:24 enjoins Israelites not to behave like a moneylender but to give interest-free loans to the poor, which sounds more like exhortation to charity than a legal prohibition. Leviticus 25:35–38 directly forbids interest, but in very special circumstances (see below). The broadest provision is Deuteronomy 23:20, which forbids interest on loans to one's "brother" (i.e., an Israelite) but permits it on loans to foreigners.

There is some evidence for the existence of antichretic pledge. A person referred to as a "resident" (*tošab*—pronounced "toe-shahv") is of a low socioeconomic status and often associated in the Torah with the resident alien and the hireling (Exod. 12:45; Lev. 25:6, 40). Leviticus 25:35–37 describes the situation where a fellow Israelite has fallen into debt and is living with his creditor as a "resident alien and resident" (*ger we-tošab*). That is exactly the circumstances of an antichretic pledge, in which the debtor lives with the creditor and works, in lieu of paying interest on his debt. The biblical law forbids the charging of interest on his debt or on his food rations. That would amount to interest upon interest, since he is already paying through his labor.

Other provisions on pledge in the Torah are concerned to restrict its application to movables, such as garments, for reasons of social welfare. Evidently such pledges were taken on subsistence loans to the very poorest and could easily be abused (Amos 2:8). Thus it is forbidden to take a millstone or a widow's garment in pledge (Deut. 24:6, 17). If a garment is pledged, the creditor must return it before sunset (Exod. 22:25–26; Deut. 24:12–13). This curious provision, which would seem to negate the purpose of the pledge, is the same as we saw above for a hired day laborer's wages. It may therefore have been intended for the same situation: a subsistence loan was given in the morning, to be paid for by a day's labor, which in turn was secured by the surrender of the laborer's garment. The only sanction is divine, after an appeal to God by the victim, but it may reflect the real possibility of a plea to an official of abuse of power. It has been suggested that similar circumstances may lie behind the Yavneh Yam Inscription, which is a plea for the return of a wrongfully withheld garment.

Finally, it is forbidden to enter a debtor's house to seize his pledge. The creditor must wait outside while the debtor brings it out to him (Deut. 24:10–11). The circumstances may be forfeiture of a pledge when the debtor is unable to repay the loan.

Forfeiture might involve all the debtor's property (Ps. 109:11–12), a situation contemplated in hypothecary pledges from Mesopotamia. Where a debtor has died leaving his widow unable to pay the debt, the creditor is entitled to take her children as debt-slaves. The solution is not to challenge the validity of the creditor's right but to provide the widow with the means to repay the loan (2 Kgs. 4:1–7).

The common use of sureties (guarantors) is attested by repeated warnings in Proverbs about the foolishness of standing surety for an outsider—apparently anyone outside one's own family, even a neighbor (Prov. 6:1–3; 11:15; 17:18). Suretyship involved a ceremony in which the surety struck the hand of the debtor (Prov. 6:1; 17:18; 22:26). Sometimes not even a surety was sufficient security, for the creditor might demand a pledge, such as a garment, from the surety himself (Prov. 20:16). Consequently the surety is warned that on forfeiture they may even take his bed from under him (Prov. 22:26–27).

Two other loans are recorded that are entirely different in nature from the loans described above. In Genesis 38:17–18, Judah defers payment for a prostitute's services, promising to send her a kid from his flock. As a pledge, he gives her his seal, sash, and staff, which serve more as evidence for the loan than as security for default. Exodus 22:13–14 regulates a loan for use. Unlike the loans above, where repayment is the same quantity of whatever commodity was loaned, in this case the very object entrusted to the borrower, such as an animal, is to be returned after use. The law rules that if the animal is killed or injured while in the borrower's care, he must compensate the lender.

E. Betrothal

Betrothal has already been discussed in the chapter on marriage as stage one in the formation of marriage. It is an agreement to give the bride to the groom in marriage—an important form of contract in the ancient systems. The betrothal contract may include a promise to pay to the bride's family an agreed sum (called *mohar* in the Bible).

The contract is concluded between the parents or guardians of the bride and the groom himself, or between both sets of parents. Thus Abraham's servant negotiates on Abraham's behalf an agreement with Laban regarding Abraham's son and Laban's sister (Gen. 24). When Samson falls in love with a Philistine woman, he asks his mother and father to make the contract for him with her father (Judg. 14:1–5). In the same manner, Hamor negotiates a contract with the father and brothers of Dinah at the request of his son Shechem

(Gen. 34:8–12). Jacob, on the other hand, deals directly with Laban, as does David with Saul (Gen. 29:15–28; 1 Sam. 18:17–27).

When it is still at the stage of promises, it is not clear how binding the agreement is: Saul makes an agreement with David to give him his daughter Merab but then reneges, without further consequences (1 Sam. 18:17–18). Occasional references in ancient Near East sources suggest that the promise could be strengthened with an oath. A clause in a contract from Larsa from the eighteenth century states (no. 51 in Faust 1941):

> Dashuratum swore the oath of King Rim-Sin: "Henceforth, be it for five years or ten, I shall keep my daughter for Ellulum, and I shall indeed give her to him in marriage."

Betrothal is turned into a real contract when the agreed bridal payment is made to the bride's parents. Throughout the ancient Near East, this payment is usually in silver, more rarely in goods. The biblical narratives, however, recount only unusual payments in the form of services. Jacob agrees to work seven years as a shepherd as payment for Rachel (Gen. 29:15–28); he bases his demand for fulfillment of the contract on the completion of his term (v. 21). Othniel captures an enemy city for his father-in-law Caleb (Judg. 1:12–13). Likewise, David performs a deed of military prowess by way of payment to Saul for his daughter Michal (1 Sam. 18:22–27).

F. Partnership

The most bizarre contract in the Bible is reported in 2 Kings 6:25–31. During the siege of Samaria, two women agree to cook and eat each other's sons on successive days. The first mother complains to the king that she fulfilled her part of the bargain, but that the other mother then hid her son to prevent his being eaten. As gruesome as the story is, from a legal point of view, the contract is best described as a form of partnership for a specific purpose.

2. PROMISSORY OATH

In the Bible, the promissory oath is an oath sworn in the name of God (YHWH) to do or to abstain from doing something in the future. For this reason promissory oaths are the basis of international treaties, which normally consist of future promises (e.g., Josh. 9:1–21). Treaties are not part of a separate system of international law, as in the modern world, but simply contracts entered into by rulers on behalf of their subjects, just as a father could contract on behalf of his family. While they can in theory be spontaneous acts (1 Sam. 19:6), most oaths are adjured; that is, the beneficiary stipulates a certain act or omission on the part of the promissor, to which the latter swears. Strictly speaking, witnesses are superfluous, since the deity is a witness, but it would be advantageous to have witnesses to prove the existence of an oath if its breach is to be punished by human hand.

Promissory oaths are not regulated in the law codes of the Torah, and most of the examples in the narratives relate to unusual situations. The closest to everyday life is the oath that Nehemiah obtains from creditors to forgo the debts owed them by fellow Jews and to restore pledges (Neh. 5:11–12). To emphasize the solemnity of the oath, Nehemiah brings in priests as witnesses. Abraham makes his slave his agent for concluding a marriage contract for his son. He adjures the slave to fulfill certain conditions in carrying out his commission (Gen. 24:1–9). While a contract can be made between slave and owner, as examples from the ancient Near East testify, strictly speaking, it is not necessary, since the slave is bound to obey his master's instructions. On the other hand, Abraham is old and may die before completion of the commission, which is to be carried out abroad, outside the scope of Abraham's jurisdiction. Under those circumstances, Abraham is wise to obtain the extra security of a divine sanction. More exotic contracts are those of Joseph with his brothers, whom he adjures to take his bones with them when they eventually leave Egypt (Gen. 50:25; Exod. 13:19), and of Rahab the prostitute with the Israelite spies, whom she adjures to ensure the safety of herself and her family when the Israelites take Jericho (Josh. 2:12–14). While Rahab uses her act of concealing the spies as grounds for the contract, it is not a real contract, because her act was not based on a prior agreement. The legal basis of a contract is not always spelled out in the narratives: King Solomon makes Shimei promise not to leave the area of Jerusalem, where he is under house arrest (1 Kgs. 2:36–38). Only later, when Shimei breaks his promise, do we learn that it was in the form of a solemn oath (vv. 42–46).

The oath has the advantage (or disadvantage) of being highly formalistic and rigid. Once made, it cannot be broken, even if obtained by deception or unfairly. The Gibeonites take advantage of this characteristic to obtain a peace treaty with the Israelites (Josh. 9:1–21). When Jacob demands Esau's birthright in return for a bowl of soup, he does not rely on the real contract and the fact of his having fulfilled his side of the bargain, but insists on making Esau's promise more secure by adjuring him first (Gen. 25:29–34).

If the promissor considers that there are conditions under which the oath should not be binding, it is advisable to spell them out. Thus the spies obtain the assent of Rahab that they will be free of their oath if she or her family subsequently disclose the spies' mission or fail to follow the instructions on what to do during the taking of the city (Josh. 2:17–21). Similarly, Abraham's slave obtains from his master the statement that he will be released from his oath if the chosen bride does not consent to follow him (Gen. 24:8).

The oath is essentially a unilateral contract. It can be made to resemble a bilateral contract through reciprocal oaths, but it is not clear how far the obligations are made dependent on each other thereby. Examples of reciprocal oaths include a peace treaty between Isaac and Abimelech (Gen. 26:26–31) and a contract between David and Jonathan (1 Sam. 18:3; 20:8, 42). The terms of the latter contract are not spelled out, but it would seem to be against harming each other or their families. Because of the oaths, Jonathan does not hand over David to Saul (1 Sam. 20:8), and David spares Jonathan's son Mephibosheth (1 Sam. 21:7). David had also made an oath to Saul with the same content (1 Sam. 24:21–22).

3. SOCIAL JUSTICE

Debt was a chronic social problem throughout the ancient world. In an economy based on agriculture, credit was necessary to ensure a supply of seed grain and to tide farmers over the lean period before harvest. Natural disasters such as drought, flood, and disease, compounded with the devastations of war, meant that sometimes farmers could not repay their loans. They would then be forced to sell off family land to satisfy creditors and, if that were insufficient, to sell their families and even themselves into slavery. A contract from Emar illustrates the process (no. 215 in Arnaud 1986):

> Before the elders of the city of Uri, Dagan-belu son of Ashada stated thus: "I was indebted for 100 shekels of silver, and Ba'al-malik son of Ba'al-qarrad the divination priest has paid my debts. In exchange for my debts that he has paid for me, I, together with my two wives—and whatever inheritance share in the orchard that I have with my brothers and my fields—have entered into slavery with Ba'al-malik of my own free will." This is the silver for which he entered: seventy shekels given to Ibni-Dagan son of Dagan-talih, ten shekels given to Itur-Dagan son of Iddid-ahu, twenty shekels given to Hila'u son of Arib-sharri.
>
> (seven witnesses)

If land or persons were pledged, forfeiture of the pledge had the same result, being expressed as a form of forced sale. An example from fourteenth-century Assyria reads (no. 12 in Ebeling 1927):

> Siniya son of Shimi-nada and Amur-dannussa son of Iqish-Ea have received seventeen mina of tin, by the city-hall weight, from

> Iddin-Kubi son of Rish-Nabu. They shall repay the capital of the tin within four months.
>
> Iddin-Kubi will hold as security for this tin five *iku* of their good-quality field in the meadow of the town of Guppi-Ekallim. If the due date passes, their field is acquired and taken; they have received the tin, the price of their field. They are paid, quit.
>
> They shall clear the field [of claims], measure it with the king's rope, and write a confirmation tablet before the king. Until they write a confirmation tablet, this [tablet] is confirmation. (six witnesses. Date)

Landlessness and enslavement of a formerly free class could have grave consequences for the social equilibrium of a society. Ancient rulers took steps to relieve the burden of debt and restore social equilibrium. Their actions were seen as a religious as well as a political duty, an important part of the divine mandate that a ruler received and that legitimized his rule—to do justice. In practical terms, it meant radical interventions in the economic life of the society and compromising an essential economic function of the law: to create predictability in commercial dealings. In terms of legal theory, it negated a fundamental premise of contract law, that a legal contract turns a bargain into a set of strict, irreversible obligations for the parties. Accordingly, rulers and law courts proceeded with caution, hedging the principles of social justice with conditions and restrictions, which varied from system to system.

There were three levels of intervention:

1. The courts allowed family property sold outright because of debt to be treated as if it were a still valid pledge and to be redeemable on payment of the debt. The court looked behind the formality of sale at the reality of the transaction, namely, the forfeiture of a pledge. Although the principle was universal, each legal system applied it sparingly to special circumstances. Thus LE 39 rules:

> If a man grows weak and sells his house, the day the buyer will sell, the owner of the house may redeem.

"Grows weak" is a technical expression for inability to repay one's debts. In the case of persons, LH 119 provides:

> If a debt seizes a man and he sells his female slave who has borne him children, the slave owner may pay the silver that the merchant paid and redeem his slave.

A measure of the pragmatism of redemption provisions is the ruling of the government of Assur (eighteenth century) to allow Assyrians who had been forced by debt to sell their paternal house to redeem them by a down payment of half the sale price, the balance payable in three annual installments (no. 46 in Michel and Garelli 1997).

2. Limits were set on the term of service of a debt-slave. Again, although in theory the slave had been purchased outright, freedom was automatic after a few years. The underlying premise was that the slave's labor had by then paid off the debt and its interest. According to LL 14,

> If a man has returned his slavery to his master and it is confirmed (that he has done so) twofold, that slave shall be released.

The term limit could be fixed, as in CH 117:

> If a debt seizes a man and he sells his wife, son, and daughter, or hands them over as a penalty, they shall serve in the house of their purchaser or penalty-holder for three years; in the fourth year their freedom shall be established.

3. The ruler personally decreed a general cancellation of debts and the return of property and persons pledged or sold because of those debts. This radical measure, akin to the amnesties sometimes proclaimed by modern governments, was most commonly exercised on the accession of a new monarch to the throne. It could, however, be occasioned by other events: a crisis such as famine or war, or a petition from citizens. The Hittite king Tudhaliya mentions just such a petition in the introduction to his debt-release decree (see the edition in Westbook and Woodard 1990):

> When I had destroyed Assuwa and returned to Hattusa, I refurbished the gods; the men of Hatti all began to bow down to me, and they spoke as follows: O great king, you are our lord, a leader of campaigns; are you not able to judge in matters of justice?

Several examples of such decrees have survived from the ancient Near East, showing the complexity of their provisions, which distinguish, for example, between the debt of common people and of merchants (the latter was not canceled), and between citizens and noncitizens (the latter did not benefit from the decree). An example is the Edict of King Ammi-ṣaduqa of Babylon §20 (see the edition in Kraus 1984):

> If a freeman of Numhia, a freeman of Emut-balum, a freeman of Idamaraz, a freeman of Uruk, a freeman of Isin, a freeman of Kisurra, or a freeman of Murgu is bound by a debt and sells himself, his wife, or his children, or hands them over as a pledge or a penalty: because the king has established justice for the land, he is released—his freedom is established.

The same principles as in the ancient Near East are found in early Greek and Roman law, but a hostility to debt-slavery for citizens ultimately led to its abolition altogether. Thus we are told that Solon not only decreed a cancellation of debts and the freeing of debt-slaves, but abolished debt-slavery henceforth (Aristotle, *Athenaion Politeia* 6.1; Plutarch, *Solon* 15.3). The use of the person of the debtor as security for a debt was abolished in Roman law by the Lex Poetelia at the end of the fourth century. Diodorus Siculus, a Hellenistic writer, attributes the same measure to Bocchoris (Bakenrenef), an eighth-century Pharaoh, but this may be a projection back into time of contemporary attitudes (*Biblioteca Historica* I 270–73).

In looking at the biblical laws, we should remember that they draw heavily upon the older traditions of the ancient Near East but also show signs of changes in the conception of debt-slavery that were emerging in the societies of the Mediterranean basin in the mid–first millennium. The biblical laws create a unique structure, or rather structures, since they reflect differing ideologies within ancient Israel. It is also in this area that the most pressing questions arise as to the relationship of the biblical laws to everyday practice. Some of the rules are strikingly utopian. Apart from prohibitions on interest and certain types of security that we have already seen, the three levels of intervention are in evidence:

1. Redemption is regulated in Leviticus 25, as part of the social welfare laws of the Priestly source. Redemption of agricultural land is available in the same circumstances as in LE 39: "if your brother grows weak . . ." (Lev. 25:23–27). In other words, this is where sale is forced upon the owner by debt. If the owner has not the means to redeem the land, then the right falls to the nearest relative.

Redemption is a right, to be exercised for the redeemer's own benefit. The purpose is to keep land in the family, not necessarily in the hands of the original owner. As is pointed out in Jeremiah 32:8, the redeemer is also the next heir to the property. He is therefore protecting his own interest. In Ruth 4:3–8, the closest relative refuses to redeem Elimelech's land because in the complicated circumstances of the narrative, it might be to his financial disadvantage. He therefore cedes his right to the next heir in line, by ceremonially removing his sandal and handing it to Boaz.

Special limitations apply to houses in walled cities, which are redeemable only for a year after purchase (Lev. 25:29–30). Houses in unwalled villages and houses owned by Levites are expressly excluded from this limitation and are treated like agricultural land (vv. 31–32).

Redemption of debt-slaves follows the same pattern. It applies only to an Israelite in debt-slavery and not to a resident alien, because in P's system, an Israelite enslaved by a fellow Israelite is to be treated like a hired laborer or an antichretic pledge, while a foreign slave is entitled to no social justice measures but may be treated as property (Lev. 25:39–49).

Although included in a wider social program and embossed with moral exhortation, the redemption laws of the Torah are pragmatic measures rooted in everyday life, no different from those found among Israel's neighbors. They are directed not to the poor as such but to established families fallen upon hard times.

In the prophetical writings and in the Greek Bible (New Testament), redemption becomes a powerful metaphor in describing relations between God and humans. It is used for various theological concepts ranging from the political fate of the nation and the state of an individual's soul. The metaphor, however, has humble origins—in a practical institution designed to temper the consequences of temporary indebtedness.

2. Term limits on debt slavery are found in two codes of the Torah, Misphatim and Deuteronomy. In both the limit is six years and benefits only Hebrew slaves, but they differ in some details.

Exodus 21:2–6 contemplates the possibility of the debt-slave receiving a bride from his owner. The law considers only a male slave, while Exodus 21:7–11 expressly excludes female slave concubines. Deuteronomy 15:12–18 applies equally to male and female slaves. Verse 18 rationalizes the term limit by pointing out that the slave has served twice the term of a hired laborer, a rationale that reflects the principle of LL 14 above. A three-year term, as we have seen, was a traditional period of hire. It is also the term laid down in CH 117 above.

Both laws allow the slave to opt to remain in permanent slavery at the end of his term. In Exodus, the motive is partly the male slave's wife, whom his master gave him in marriage and will not be released with him. Deuteronomy applies the option to both male and female slaves.

3. The practice of a general cancellation of debts was known in Israel. Nehemiah, as leader of the community of Jews returned from exile, coerces creditors into canceling debts held against their fellow Jews (Neh. 5:9–13). During the siege of Jerusalem by the Babylonian army, King Zedekiah decrees the release of Hebrew debt-slaves (Jer. 34:8–10).

Like royal decrees elsewhere, the decrees of Nehemiah and Zedekiah are an exercise of the ruler's discretion, the timing of which cannot be predicted. It is exactly these qualities that make a general debt release a practical measure. If it were predictable, credit would cease to be available, since no one willingly makes a loan that he is sure will not be repaid. The relevant laws of the Torah, however, are cyclical and therefore predictable.

Deuteronomy 15:1–3 decrees a release every seventh year. It recognizes that this will lead creditors to withhold loans and exhorts them to be generous (vv. 9–10). Leviticus 25 institutes the jubilee year every fiftieth year: land is to be restored to its owners, and all Israelite slaves are to be released (in conjunction with a fallow year based on a seven-year fallow cycle). It superimposes the jubilee on the regulations regarding redemption of land and slaves, so that they all become relative. (This source knows nothing of term limits on debt slavery.) Whatever their effect, land and slaves cannot be sold for more than fifty years, and the price of redemption will be calculated by the time remaining to the next jubilee year. What is being sold is a number of harvests or years of hired labor.

There is no evidence that the sabbatical or jubilee years were ever imposed in practice. In the postbiblical period the Rabbis, while obliged to obey the letter of the Torah, recognized their impracticality and took steps to avert their effects. Hillel invented the Prosbol, a declaration before the court regarding a debt that allowed the creditor to reclaim payment in disregard of the sabbatical year (Mishnah, *Shabbat* 10:2).

The sabbatical and jubilee laws appear to emanate from circles that had no faith in kings' exercising their discretion to enact measures of social justice. The aftermath of King Zedekiah's debt release explains why. The owners subsequently reenslaved their debt-slaves (Jer. 34:10–11). The prophet Jeremiah berated them by citing an old slave-release law that they had purportedly neglected (v. 14):

> Every seventh year each one of you shall release his Hebrew brother who was sold to you; when he has served you six years you shall send him free . . .

The contradiction in the text cited between a general release and an individual term limit reflects an attempt to amalgamate the two different laws found in Deuteronomy 15, to turn the decision of an individual into a regular cyclical event that did not depend on the frailty of political leaders. The solution, however, created a legal institution that could function only in utopia, not in everyday Israel.

Further Reading

Some titles have been abbreviated; see bibliography for full citations.

Chirichigno, G. 1993. *Debt-Slavery in Israel and the Ancient Near East*: chap. 6: The Manumission Laws of Exodus 21.2–6, 7–11 (186–255); chap. 7: The Manumission Law of Deuteronomy 15.12–18 (256–301); chap. 8: The Manumission Law of Leviticus 25.39–43, 47–55 (302–43).

Daube, D. 1947. *Studies in Biblical Law*, 3–24.

Finkelstein, J. J. 1968. "An Old Babylonian Herding Contract and Genesis 31:38f.," 30–36.

Frymer-Kensky, T. 2001. "Israel," in *Security for Debt*, 251–63.
Gamoran, H. 1971. "The Biblical Law against Loans on Interest," 127–34.
Maloney, R. P. 1974. "Usury and Restrictions on Interest-Taking," 1–20.
Miller, G. P. 1993. "Contracts in Genesis," 15–45.
Postgate, J. N. 1975. "Some Old Babylonian Shepherds and Their Flocks," 1–21.
Tucker, G. M. 1966a. "The Legal Background of Genesis 23," 77–84.
Viberg, Å. 1992. *Symbols of Law*, 45–51, 145–65.
Westbrook, R. 1991. *Property and the Family*: chap. 1: Purchase of the Cave of Machpelah (24–35); chap. 2: Jubilee Laws (36–57); chap. 3: Redemption of Land (58–68); chap. 5: The Price Factor in the Redemption of Land (90–117).
Yadin, Y. 1962. "Expedition D: The Cave of Letters," 235–37.
Yaron, R. 1959. "Redemption of Persons in the Ancient Near East," 155–76.

Questions for Review

1. Which of the following statements best describes a "real contract"?
   a. an agreement between two parties in which they bind themselves to their obligations by means of an oath
   b. an agreement between two parties where both parties still have to fulfill their obligations
   c. an agreement between two parties where both parties have obligations but where one party has already fulfilled its obligations
   d. an agreement between two parties where only one party has obligations
2. Why does the story in Genesis 23 have Abraham insisting that he pay the full price for the land that he buys, even though the owner of the land offers to give it to Abraham free of charge?
   a. If Abraham had not paid the full market price, the owner's heirs could later reclaim the land and buy it back at the price that Abraham had paid.
   b. The narrative wants to portray Abraham as generous in his business dealings.
   c. In the story, Abraham wants to create goodwill between himself and the Hittites because he wants to settle in their land.
   d. Abraham had originally agreed to pay full price for the land and did not want to be seen as going back on his word.
3. What type of worker in biblical Israel was considered to hold a status that, in economic terms, was not much above that of a slave?
   a. shepherds on yearly contracts
   b. wet nurses
   c. day laborers
   d. conscripted soldiers
4. In which of the following situations must a shepherd replace animals entrusted to the shepherd by their owner?
   a. when they have been taken or killed by wild, predatory animals
   b. when they have been stolen
   c. when they have died from sickness or some other apparently natural cause

5. Which of the following types of pledge identifies a situation where the lender (creditor) is allowed to profit from the pledge—for example, by using the pledged field, by putting the pledged person to work—but where that profit takes the place of any interest that might otherwise have to be paid?
   a. hypothecary pledge
   b. antichretic pledge
   c. possessory pledge
6. Which of the following statements best describes the attitude of biblical legal texts toward the charging of interest on loans?
   a. The texts of the Hebrew Bible are clear in that they strictly prohibit the charging of any interest on loans.
   b. The texts of the Hebrew Bible treat the charging of interest as a normal part of business dealings, as do other ancient Near Eastern legal texts.
   c. The texts of the Hebrew Bible are mixed, with the Priestly source forbidding interest and other sources tolerating it in most cases.
   d. The texts of the Hebrew Bible are mixed, with the Priestly source forbidding interest in the case of antichretic pledge, the D source forbidding interest charged to a fellow Israelite, and other sources tolerating it.
7. What does the book of Proverbs mean when it warns readers not to act as surety for someone else's debt?
8. At what point does a betrothal agreement become a real contract?
9. Which of the following is *not* one of the ways that governments in ancient Near Eastern lands, other than Israel, would intervene in their society's economy in order to relieve problems of widespread and excessive debt?
   a. They would establish a set interval of years when they would regularly cancel debts and allow persons and property, either pledged or sold because of those debts, to return to their original families/owners.
   b. They would establish a time limit on how long a person could serve as a debt-slave. At the end of that time period, the person could return home, and the debt would be deemed paid.
   c. They would allow property that families had sold due to financial difficulty to be repurchased by those families at the same price for which they had sold it.
   d. They would issue occasional and unpredictably timed decrees that would cancel private debts and allow pledges and sold persons/items to return to their owners or families.
10. What happened, according to Jeremiah 34, shortly after King Zedekiah of Judah ordered the complete release of Hebrew debt-slaves?

Answers

1. The answer is (c).
2. The answer is (a). It was important in land-sale agreements to indicate that the "full price" had been paid if the buyer wished to avoid future claims on the land by the seller's heirs.

3. The answer is (c). Day laborers were hired for only one day and often did not know whether they would have work the next day. Biblical law requires that those who employ such laborers pay them their wages on the same day when the work is done, though no judicial penalty is prescribed for failure to do so.
4. The answer is (b). Apparently the shepherd was not liable for damage caused by wild animals. In some cases, the shepherd is to bring the remains of the dead animal to the owner as evidence of what happened (Exod. 22:12).
5. The answer is (b). The term antichretic is used of situations where no official interest is charged but where the person or property given to the lender as a pledge (or, as we might say today, as collateral) can be used by the lender. Whatever the latter gains by such use acts as compensation for the loss of any interest payment.
6. The answer is (d). Some will say that the correct answer is (a), that the Hebrew Bible forbids the charging of interest in all cases. Many popular discussions of the topic today assume that this is the case. But biblical texts present a more complicated picture. While P and D bar the charging of interest in some cases, the Covenant Code appears to allow it, yet it strongly encourages its audience not to charge interest on loans to poor Israelites, though no explicit criteria for the notion of "poor" are set forth.
7. To act as surety is very similar to being a cosigner on a loan today. The person who functions as surety for a loan guarantees that the lender will be repaid if the principal borrower fails to pay the debt on time. Such a person is often called a guarantor.
8. It becomes a real contract when the bridal payment is made by the groom or his parents and received by the bride's family. The members of the groom's family have fulfilled their contractual obligations. Now the members of the bride's family must fulfill theirs by delivering the bride at the appointed time.
9. The answer is (a). Only in the Bible do we have this type of governmental action proposed. It likely comes from those who were disappointed with their current monarchical administration and perhaps with that administration's lack of attention to matters of economic justice. The concept is so idealistic, however, that many scholars doubt whether it was ever carried out and whether it would have worked if attempted.
10. Zedekiah and all the others who had set their debt-slaves free reenslaved the very same people. One possibility is that Zedekiah and his officials implemented the release as a way to curry favor with God, when they were faced with the attacking Babylonian army having reached the environs of Jerusalem. They may then have heard a rumor that the Egyptian army was on its way to defend against the Babylonian attack. This perhaps inspired them with confidence, and they saw no more need to rely on their morality when they would soon have a mighty army at their side. As we know now, the Egyptians never made it to Jerusalem.

Conclusion

While a comprehensive knowledge of the laws of biblical Israel will always elude us, we are by no means bereft of data, and the analysis presented in this book has attempted to demonstrate that. The foregoing chapters have described in significant detail the important components of ancient Israel's legal system—components, such as litigation, inheritance rights, and contract law, that are important for any system of law to function well. The breadth of description and the level of detail have been achieved by two primary means. First, we took an explicitly legal approach to the texts of the Hebrew Bible, principally the law codes of the Pentateuch. Other approaches—whether literary or social-scientific or the like—can certainly function as valid ways of reading these texts, but the discovery of law comes through using the kind of analysis and categories that legal scholars would apply to most legal systems. We also took this approach with other biblical genres, although caution had to be exercised in this regard, since a genre such as narrative will sometimes distort the law it uses for dramatic purposes. Second, we placed the biblical material within the context of ancient Israel's neighbors—primarily those from the ancient Near East, but also those from the early Mediterranean world. One finds in these societies a collection of legal systems that shared numerous practices, institutions, and modes of reasoning, and of which biblical law formed a definite part. In this way, a number of gaps within our knowledge of Israel's system have been filled in to provide a fuller picture of law in biblical Israel.

For most scholars, however, the study of biblical law does not stop here. A number of questions remain to be answered about the legal texts of the Bible. Two of the most important are the following:

1. What is the relationship between the biblical law codes and the narratives into which they have been placed?
2. What is the relationship between the biblical law codes themselves?

There is no especially obvious connection, for example, between the provisions of the Covenant Code and the larger story surrounding it of the Israelites' journey from Egypt and stay at Mount Sinai. Moreover, as demonstrated in previous chapters, there are occasional points of tension, if not contradiction, between the biblical law codes. The legal approach taken in this book is insufficient on its own to address all the important issues arising from these problems. Nevertheless, when combined with other reliable methods, a legal analysis informed by evidence from ancient Near Eastern and Mediterranean societies other than Israel is a necessary step toward finding viable solutions. By way of conclusion, then, we offer a brief perspective on these issues.

To begin with, it is very likely that the biblical codes—the Covenant Code and large sections of the Deuteronomic Code in particular—were not originally part of a larger narrative. They were probably stand-alone codes or collections of law just as those from the cuneiform tradition. As explained in chapter 1, the law codes come from the ancient Near Eastern scribal practice of compiling lists. Scribes appear to have assembled all sorts of lists (omens, medical symptoms, etc.), and the law codes fall into this category. The Laws of Hammurabi, for instance, almost certainly had nothing to do with King Hammurabi originally. The provisions contained in the code were compiled and/or composed by scribes. What LH shows us is that such lists of laws could be used for purposes other than those initially envisioned by the scribes who authored them. In the case of LH and others (e.g., LU, LL), the lists/codes became tools for royal propaganda. They were lifted out of their original, scribal-academic context and inserted into an entirely different context: the royal inscription. They were then framed by explicitly propagandistic prologues and epilogues to give them the look and feel of royal proclamation. The laws and rules of these codes were meant to illustrate how well the king, in whose name they were published, had established justice throughout his realm.

Analogous reasoning can be applied to the biblical codes (Westbrook 1994b). For example, agricultural laws in the Covenant Code (e.g., Exod. 22:4–5) belie the narrative setting where the people are on a journey through a desert region and receive daily amounts of manna for food. In all likelihood, this code too has been taken from its scribal setting and given a role to play in a larger story, of which it was never initially a part. Instead of being used for royal propaganda, however, this code has been put to use for religious purposes. The narrative frame surrounding it focuses on the agreement or covenant established between God and Israel at Mount Sinai. Such agreements between human entities—city-states, for instance—typically included a list of specific stipulations by which the weaker of the two parties had to abide. It appears that the rules of the Covenant Code fulfill this function for the narrative as it has come down to us in the book of Exodus. That is, the code contains the specific rules that the authors of this section of Exodus wanted to be associated with the Sinai covenant. For the people of Israel to keep their covenantal obligations, claim the authors, they had to obey the provisions of this code.

A similar explanation works as well for the list of laws in Deuteronomy—the Deuteronomic Code. In Deuteronomy, however, there seem to be two covenants in view. The text certainly looks back to a covenant that is either identical or similar to the Sinai covenant (e.g., Deut. 5:2). Deuteronomy refers to the place where this covenant was established as Horeb rather than Sinai, and scholars disagree as to whether these toponyms refer to the same or different places. The book also identifies a new covenant, a covenant made "in the land of Moab" that is "in addition to" the one made at Horeb (Deut. 28:69). As the book of Deuteronomy stands now, the laws that form the Deuteronomic Code are likely meant to function as the specific rules associated with both covenants, though that may well be debatable. In either case, the law code has once again been inserted into a covenantal context—a context that is probably not original to the code.[1]

The real question then becomes why the authors of Exodus and Deuteronomy chose these particular codes to insert into their narratives and to what degree they may have modified these codes upon insertion. One might well ask how the goring-ox laws correspond to the nature and purpose of the Sinai covenant, or how the laws on sexual relations fit with the religious goals of the authors of Deuteronomy. These are questions best left to source-critical scholars and historians of the religion of Israel (e.g., Otto 2007). Nonetheless, understanding the law-code tradition from which the biblical codes come, as well as the meaning of the individual laws, is an important prerequisite for any attempt to examine these larger questions.

As for the relationship between the law codes, this is a question that has occupied a great deal of recent scholarship on biblical law. It has been argued by a number of scholars that the authors of the Deuteronomic Code were aware of the provisions of the Covenant Code and drew some of their ideas therefrom. There is disagreement, however, regarding the purpose behind this use of the

1. It is considerably more difficult to apply this sort of reasoning to the laws in Leviticus that come from the Priestly source. Although they contain laws that have secular counterparts among neighboring systems, such as those regarding female inheritance, the character of most of these laws, and not just their context, is much more religious than that of the laws in the Covenant and Deuteronomic codes. The likelihood therefore exists that the authors of the Priestly source wrote many of these laws themselves rather than obtaining them from a list or code that had been created earlier.

Covenant Code. Were the authors of the Deuteronomic Code attempting to revise and even overturn the Covenant Code (Levinson 1997)? Or did they accept its basic authority and were only reinterpreting it for a new time and new challenges (Otto 1996)? Regardless of which view one takes, it is important that sound legal analysis be applied to each code's individual provisions. If a provision in one code is indeed using material from a provision in another code, it stands to reason that knowing the legal meaning and import of each provision is necessary to understanding how the one makes use of the other.

The slave laws from Exodus and Deuteronomy provide a useful illustration. Previous scholarship has often liked to point out that a significant difference exists in the way the two codes treat female debt-slaves (Ska 2006). In the Covenant Code, for example, male debt-slaves are allowed to go free after six years of service (Exod. 21:2). But only a few verses later the code states: "When a man sells his daughter as a slave, she shall not go out as the male slaves do" (Exod. 21:7). This is usually interpreted to mean that female slaves will not be able to leave the master's household in the seventh year. On the other hand, the Deuteronomic Code contains a provision that gives both male and female debt-slaves the chance to go free after serving the creditor for six years (Deut. 15:12; see the discussion in chapter 6). This has led in part to the general idea that the Deuteronomic Code treats women in a much more positive way: it is attempting to revise previous law, such as that contained in the Covenant Code, in order to grant women legal rights equal to those of men (e.g., Phillips 1984).

The problem with this line of reasoning is its assumption that the law in Exodus 21:7–11, concerning female debt-slaves, has to do with an ordinary debt-slave arrangement in the same manner as the law concerning male debt-slaves in Exodus 21:2–6. As discussed in chapter 4, a careful reading of Exodus 21:7–11 shows that this is manifestly not the case. The purpose of the sale is concubinage. The law assumes a situation where a father is deeply in debt and is forced to sell his daughter. In order to provide her with extra legal protection, he arranges for her sale not merely as a debt-slave but as a concubine, a slave-wife. Because a special purpose lies behind the sale, this law does not speak to the issue of an ordinary debt-slave arrangement. In fact, the Covenant Code does not deal at all with regular female debt-slaves. How the code's authors believed such slaves should normally be handled is not disclosed. Thus the alleged difference between the Covenant Code and the Deuteronomic Code in this regard is more apparent than real, and a conclusion in favor of a kinder approach to women in Deuteronomy is unwarranted, at least on the basis of these two provisions.

In the end, the precise nature of the relationship between the codes remains unclear. Most scholars believe that the Covenant Code was the earlier to be compiled, and recent work has made a strong case that the authors of the Deuteronomic Code, which came next, knew the earlier code and that the Priestly authors knew both (Stackert 2007). Whether one should expect later codes to seek to undermine earlier ones or whether the later authors hoped readers would see a legal harmony among the different codes is still debated. That all of these codes were deemed fit for biblical Israel's canon of sacred texts is another factor that scholarship must take into account.

To be sure, many aspects of biblical law will continue to be debated. Not only the larger historical and interpretive questions alluded to here, but also detailed points of law relating to individual provisions, will no doubt come under ever greater scrutiny. And, as more discoveries come to light from the ancient Near Eastern and Mediterranean worlds, our understanding will go on being enlarged and refined. Even so, as scholarship on biblical law moves forward into the future, a key ingredient of its enterprise will remain the kind of analysis that has been presented here—an analysis that can help to reconstruct the everyday law of biblical Israel.

Further Reading

Some titles have been abbreviated; see bibliography for full citations.

Levinson, B. M. 1997. *Deuteronomy and the Hermeneutics of Legal Innovation*, 3–22.
Otto, E. 1996. "The Pre-exilic Deuteronomy as a Revision of the Covenant Code," 112–22.
———. 2007. "The Pivotal Meaning of Pentateuch Research for a History of Israelite and Jewish Religion and Society," 29–53.
Phillips, A. 1984. "The Laws of Slavery: Exodus 21.2–11," 51–66.
Ska, J. L. 2006. *Introduction to Reading the Pentateuch*, 40–52.
Stackert, J. R. 2007. *Rewriting the Torah*, 209–25.
Westbrook, R. 1994b. "What Is the Covenant Code?" 13–34.

Glossary of Legal Terms

The following are modern legal terms that have been used in the book to explain ancient legal institutions.

antichretic. A form of pledge in which the creditor holds the pledge (e.g., land or persons) and takes the income from the pledge (rent or labor) in lieu of interest on the loan.

capital (crime/punishment). For which the punishment is death.

damages. A sum of money payable to the victim as redress for the victim's loss or suffering.

delict. A wrong committed by a person against another person (other than breach of contract), for which the court may impose compensation or punishment.

dispositive. Describes evidence, such as a document, that is not merely evidence of a legal transaction but has the effect of a legal transaction on its own, for example, a will. Opposite: evidentiary.

estate. 1. Property in the form of land; 2. the property of a deceased person that passes by inheritance.

evidentiary. Describes evidence, such as a document or statement or object, that proves the existence of a past event. Opposite: dispositive.

guarantor. A person who agrees to fulfill the obligation of another named person (the "principal"), if that person fails to do so.

hypothecary. A form of pledge in which the debtor retains control of the pledge until repayment is due. The creditor may take the pledge only on the debtor's failure to repay the loan. Opposite: possessory.

intestate. Where a person dies without leaving a will and the heirs are determined by general rules of law, usually according to how closely they were related to the deceased.

judicial. By or relating to judges.

juridical. Relating to law as a scientific discipline.

jurisprudence. The science or theoretical study of law.

pecuniary. In the form of money, for example, a pecuniary penalty.

penal. Focused on punishing the culprit rather than compensating the victim.

pledge. Something belonging to the debtor that the creditor may exploit (e.g., by sale or use) to recoup the sum owed if the debtor fails to repay.

possessory. A type of pledge that the creditor holds from the granting of the loan until its repayment. Opposite: hypothecary.

precedent. A decision by a court or legal authority, the principle of which remains valid for cases with analogous facts in the future.

sanction. Penalty.

security. Means by which creditors can be satisfied that they will get their money back if the debtor cannot or will not repay the loan, for example, pledge, surety.

surety. Guarantor.

tenure. Mode in which land is held, for example, permanent ownership, for life, by lease, or by royal grant.

tort. A wrong for which redress is a private matter for the victim, not the state. Opposite: crime. NB: a delict can describe a crime or a tort.

vested. Giving rights that are already secure and not conditional on the future act or decision of another person.

vicarious punishment. Punishment that is imposed not upon the culprit but upon another person who stands in a particular relationship to the culprit, for example, employer, father, or son.

Bibliography

This bibliography includes all of the works cited in the foregoing chapters. It also includes a number of other books and articles that can be helpful when taking the kind of legal approach adopted in this book. For a much more comprehensive list of items related to the study of biblical law, see Welch 2005. For all entries below (except Welch 2005), we have indicated in brackets the major topic(s) to which each entry most closely relates. These topics have been limited to the following: Sources, Litigation, Status, Family, Crimes and Delicts, Property, Inheritance, Contracts, Slavery, Marriage, Social Justice, and General Reference.

Alt, Albrecht. 1966. "The Origins of Israelite Law." In *Essays on Old Testament History and Religion*, translated by R. A. Wilson, 81–132. Oxford: Blackwell, 1966. Reprinted from "Die Ursprünge des israelitischen Rechts," in *Berichte über die Verhandlungen der Sächsischen Akademie der Wissenschaften zu Leipzig*. Philologisch-Historische Klasse 86/1. Leipzig: Hirzel, 1934. [Sources]

Amit, Yairah. 1992. "The Jubilee Law—An Attempt at Instituting Social Justice." In *Justice and Righteousness: Biblical Themes and Their Influence*, edited by H. Reventlow and Y. Hoffman, 47–59. Sheffield: Sheffield Academic Press. [Contracts]

Anderson, Jeff S. 1998. "The Social Function of Curses in the Hebrew Bible." *Zeitschrift für die alttestamentliche Wissenschaft* 110:223–38. [Crimes and Delicts]

Arnaud, Daniel. 1986. *Emar VI: Recherches au pays d'Aštata*. Vol. 3: *Textes sumériens et accadiens*. Paris: Éditions Recherche sur les Civilisations. [Sources]

Avalos, Hector. 1990. "Exodus 22:9 and Akkadian Legal Formulae." *Journal of Biblical Literature* 109:116–17. [Contracts]

Baker, David. L. 2007. "Concubines and Conjugal Rights." *Zeitschrift für altorientalische und biblische Rechtsgeschichte* 13:87–101. [Marriage]

Barmash, Pamela. 2004. "The Narrative Quandary: Cases of Law in Literature." *Vetus Testamentum* 54:1–16. [Sources]

———. 2005. *Homicide in the Biblical World*. Cambridge: Cambridge University Press. [Crimes and Delicts]

Bellefontaine, Elizabeth. 1979. "Deuteronomy 21:18–21: Reviewing the Case of the Rebellious Son." *Journal for the Study of the Old Testament* 13:13–31. [Crimes and Delicts]

Ben-Barak, Zafrira. 1979. "The Legal Background to the Restoration of Michal to David." In *Studies in the Historical Books of the Old Testament*, edited by J. A. Emerton, 15–29. Leiden: Brill. [Marriage]

———. 1981. "Meribaal and the System of Land Grants in Ancient Israel." *Biblica* 62:73–91. [Property]

———. 2006. *Inheritance by Daughters in Israel and the Ancient Near East*. Jaffa: Archaeological Center Publications. [Inheritance]

Berlin, Adele. 1987. "On the Interpretation of Psalm 133." In *Directions in Biblical Hebrew Poetry*, edited by E. R. Follis, 141–47. Journal for the Study of the Old Testament Supplement 40. Sheffield: Sheffield Academic Press. [Inheritance]

Bigger, Stephen F. 1979. "The Family Laws of Leviticus 18 in Their Setting." *Journal of Biblical Literature* 98:187–203. [Crimes and Delicts]

Boecker, Hans Jochen. 1964. *Redeformen des Rechtslebens im Alten Testament*. Wissenschaftliche Monographien zum Alten und Neuen Testament 14. Neukirchen-Vluyn: Neukirchener Verlag. [Litigation]

———. 1980. *Law and the Administration of Justice in the Old Testament and Ancient East*. Translated by J. Moiser. London: SPCK. [Litigation]

Bord, Lucien Jean. 1997. "L'adoption dans la bible et dans le droit cunéiforme." *Zeitschrift für altorientalische und biblische Rechtsgeschichte* 3:174–94. [Family]

Bottéro, Jean. 1992. "The 'Code' of Hammurabi." In *Mesopotamia: Writing, Reasoning, and the Gods*, translated by Z. Bahrani and M. van de Mieroop, 156–84. Chicago: University of Chicago Press. [Sources]

Bovati, Pietro. 1994. *Re-Establishing Justice: Legal Terms, Concepts and Procedures in the Hebrew Bible*. Journal for the Study of the Old Testament Supplement 105. Sheffield: Sheffield Academic Press. [Litigation]

Brichto, Herbert C. 1973. "Kin, Cult, Land and Afterlife: A Biblical Complex." *Hebrew Union College Annual* 44:1–54. [Inheritance]

———. 1975. "The Case of the *Sota* and a Reconsideration of Biblical 'Law.'" *Hebrew Union College Annual* 46:55–70. [Crimes and Delicts]

Brin, Gershon. 1994. *Studies in Biblical Law: From the Hebrew Bible to the Dead Sea Scrolls*. Translated by J. Chipman. Journal for the Study of the Old Testament Supplement 176. Sheffield: Sheffield Academic Press. [Inheritance; Social Justice]

Burrows, Millar. 1938. *The Basis of Israelite Marriage*. New Haven, CT: American Oriental Society. [Family; Marriage]

Buss, Martin J. 1977. "The Distinction between Civil and Criminal Law in Ancient Israel." In *Proceedings of the 6th World Congress of Jewish Studies*, vol. 1, edited by A. Shinan, 51–62. Jerusalem: World Union of Jewish Studies. [Crimes and Delicts]

———. 1989. "Logic and Israelite Law." *Semeia* 45:49–65. [Sources]

Chirichigno, Gregory C. 1993. *Debt-Slavery in Israel and the Ancient Near East*. Journal for the Study of the Old Testament Supplement 141. Sheffield: Sheffield Academic Press. [Status; Slavery; Contracts]

Cowley, A. E., ed. 1923. *Aramaic Papyri of the Fifth Century B.C.* Oxford: Clarendon. [Sources]

Crawford, Michael H., ed. 1996. *Roman Statutes*. 2 vols. Bulletin of the Institute of Classical Studies Supplement 64. London: Institute of Classical Studies. [Sources; the Twelve Tables are in vol. 2, pp. 555–721]

Dalley, Stephanie. 1979. *A Catalogue of the Akkadian Cuneiform Tablets in the Collections of the Royal Scottish Museum, Edinburgh, with Copies of the Texts*. Royal Scottish Museum Art and Archaeology 2. Edinburgh: Royal Scottish Museum. [Sources]

Daube, David. 1947. *Studies in Biblical Law*. Cambridge: Cambridge University Press. [Sources; Inheritance; Crimes and Delicts; Contracts]

———. 1949. "Error and Accident in the Bible." *Revue Internationale des Droits de l'Antiquité* 2:189–213. [Crimes and Delicts]

———. 1950. "Consortium in Roman and Hebrew Law." *The Juridical Review* 62:71–91. [Inheritance]

———. 1986. "The Old Testament Prohibitions of Homosexuality." *Zeitschrift der Savigny-Stiftung für Rechtsgeschichte* (Romanistische Abteilung) 103:447–48. [Crimes and Delicts]

Daube, David, and Reuvon Yaron. 1956. "Jacob's Reception by Laban." *Journal of Semitic Studies* 1:60–61. [Contracts]

David, Martino. 1948. "The Manumission of Slaves under Zedekiah: A Contribution to the Laws about the Hebrew Slaves." *Oudtestamentische Studien* 5:63–79. [Status; Slavery; Contracts]

Davies, Eryl W. 1981. "Inheritance Rights and the Hebrew Levirate Marriage." *Vetus Testamentum* 31:133–44 (part 1) and 257–68 (part 2). [Inheritance]

———. 1993. "The Inheritance of the First-born in Israel and the Ancient Near East." *Journal of Semitic Studies* 38:175–91. [Inheritance]

Dearman, J. Andrew. 1988. *Property Rights in the Eighth-Century Prophets: The Conflict and Its Background.* Society of Biblical Literature Dissertation 106. Atlanta: Scholars Press. [Property; Inheritance]

Diamond, Arthur S. 1957. "An Eye for an Eye." *Iraq* 19:151–55. [Crimes and Delicts]

Dobbs-Allsopp, F. W. 1994. "The Genre of the Meṣad Ḥashavyahu Ostracon." *Bulletin of the American Schools of Oriental Research* 295:49–55. [Sources]

Doron, Pinchas. 1969. "A New Look at an Old Lex: Lex Talionis." *Journal of the Ancient Near Eastern Society of Columbia University* 1:21–27. [Crimes and Delicts]

Driver, S. R. 1902. *A Critical and Exegetical Commentary on Deuteronomy*. The International Critical Commentary on the Holy Scriptures. Edinburgh: T. & T. Clark. [General Reference]

Ebeling, Erich. 1927. *Keilschrifttexte aus Assur juristischen Inhalts*. Wissenschaftliche Veröffentlichungen der deutschen Orientgesellschaft 50. Leipzig: Hinrichs. [Sources]

Eph'al, Israel, and Joseph Naveh. 1998. "Remarks on the Recently Published Moussaieff Ostraca." *Israel Exploration Journal* 48:269–73. [Sources]

Eslinger, Lyle M. 1981. "The Case of an Immodest Lady Wrestler in Deuteronomy 25:11–12." *Vetus Testamentum* 31:269–81. [Crimes and Delicts]

Falk, Ze'ev W. 1961. "Forms of Testimony." *Vetus Testamentum* 11:88–91. [Litigation]

———. 1968. "Oral and Written Testimony." *Iura* 19:113–19. [Litigation]

———. 2001. *Hebrew Law in Biblical Times*. 2d ed. Provo, UT: Brigham Young University Press. [Sources; General Reference]

Faust, David E. 1941. *Contracts from Larsa, Dated in the Reign of Rim-Sin*. Yale Oriental Series 8. New Haven, CT: Yale University Press. [Sources]

Fensham, F. Charles. 1988. "Liability of Animals in Biblical and Ancient Near Eastern Law." *Journal of Northwest Semitic Languages* 14:85–90. [Crimes and Delicts]

Finkelstein, Jacob J. 1968. "An Old Babylonian Herding Contract and Genesis 31:38f." *Journal of the American Oriental Society* 88:30–36. [Contracts]

Fitzpatrick-McKinley, Anne. 1999. *The Transformation of Torah from Scribal Advice to Law*. Journal for the Study of the Old Testament Supplement 287. Sheffield: Sheffield Academic Press. [Sources]

Fleishman, Joseph. 1992a. "The Age of Legal Maturity in Biblical Law." *Journal of the Ancient Near Eastern Society of Columbia University* 21:35–48. [Family]

———. 1992b. "Offenses against Parents Punishable by Death: Towards a Socio-Legal Interpretation of Exodus 21:15, 17." *Jewish Law Annual* 10:7–37. [Crimes and Delicts]

———. 2000. "Does the Law of Exodus 21:7–11 Permit a Father to Sell His Daughter to Be a Slave?" *Jewish Law Annual* 13:47–64. [Slavery; Contracts]

———. 2007. "'Their Father Gave Them *nahala* "an estate" among Their Brethren' (Job 42:15b): What Did Job Give His Daughters?" *Zeitschrift für altorientalische und biblische Rechtsgeschichte* 13:120–34. [Inheritance]

Freedman, David Noel, ed. 1992. *Anchor Bible Dictionary*. 6 vols. New York: Doubleday. [General Reference]

Freedman, Leslie R. 1989. "Biblical Hebrew *'rb* 'to go surety,' and Its Nominal Forms." *Journal of the Ancient Near Eastern Society of Columbia University* 19:25–29. [Contracts]

Frymer-Kensky, Tikvah. 1980. "Tit for Tat: The Principle of Equal Retribution in Near Eastern and Biblical Law." *Biblical Archaeologist* 43:230–34. [Crimes and Delicts]

———. 1984. "The Strange Case of the Suspected Sotah (Numbers 5:11–31)." *Vetus Testamentum* 34:11–26. [Litigation]

———. 1989. "Law and Philosophy: The Case of Sex in the Bible." *Semeia* 45:89–102. [Family; Crimes and Delicts]

———. 1998. "Virginity in the Bible." In *Gender and Law in the Hebrew Bible and the Ancient Near East*, edited by V. H. Matthews, B. M. Levinson, and T. Frymer-Kensky, 79–93. Journal for the Study of the Old Testament Supplement 262. Sheffield: Sheffield Academic Press. [Family; Crimes and Delicts]

———. 2001. "Israel." In *Security for Debt in Ancient Near Eastern Law*, edited by R. Westbrook and R. Jasnow, 251–63. Culture and History of the Ancient Near East 9. Leiden: Brill. [Contracts]

Gagarin, Michael. 1986. *Early Greek Law*. Berkeley: University of California Press. [Sources]

Gamoran, Hillel. 1971. "The Biblical Law against Loans on Interest." *Journal of Near Eastern Studies* 30:127–34. [Contracts; Social Justice]

Gardiner, Alan H. 1941. "Adoption Extraordinary." *Journal of Egyptian Archaeology* 26:23–29. [Family; Inheritance]

Gertz, Jan Christian. 1994. *Die Gerichtsorganisation Israels im deuteronomischen Gesetz*. Forschungen zur Religion und Literatur des Alten und Neuen Testaments 165. Göttingen: Vandenhoeck & Ruprecht, 1994. [Sources; Litigation]

Greenberg, Moshe. 1960. "Some Postulates of Biblical Criminal Law." In *Yehezkel Kaufmann Jubilee Volume*, edited by M. Haran, 5–28. Jerusalem: Magnes. [Crimes and Delicts]

———. 1986. "More Reflections on Biblical Criminal Law." In *Studies in Bible*, edited by S. Japhet, 1–4. Scripta Hierosolymitana 11. Jerusalem: Magnes. [Crimes and Delicts]

Greengus, Samuel. 1997. "The Selling of Slaves: Laws Missing from the Hebrew Bible." *Zeitschrift für altorientalische und biblische Rechtsgeschichte* 3:1–11. [Slavery; Contracts]

Haas, Peter J. 1989. "'Die He Shall Surely Die': The Structure of Homicide in Biblical Law." *Semeia* 45:67–87. [Crimes and Delicts]

Haase, Richard. 2001. "De fetu abito sive Ne se immisceat mulier praegnans rixae inter viros: Vom ungewollten Abgang der Leibesfrucht im altorientalischen und biblischen Bereich." *Zeitschrift für altorientalische und biblische Rechtsgeschichte* 7:384–91. [Crimes and Delicts]

Hagedorn, Anselm C. 2001. "Utilising an Archaic Greek Law Code for Biblical Research." *Zeitschrift für altorientalische und biblische Rechtsgeschichte* 7:217–42. [Sources; Crimes and Delicts]

———. 2004. *Between Moses and Plato: Individual and Society in Deuteronomy and Ancient Greek Law*. Forschungen zur Religion und Literatur des Alten und Neuen Testaments 204. Göttingen: Vandenhoeck & Ruprecht. [Sources; Family; Inheritance; Crimes and Delicts]

Hiers, Richard H. 2002. "Biblical Social Welfare Legislation: Protected Classes and Provisions for Persons in Need." *Journal of Law and Religion* 17:49–96. [Social Justice]

Hoffner, Harry A., Jr. 1973. "Incest, Sodomy, and Bestiality in the Ancient Near East." In *Orient and Occident: Essays for C. H. Gordon*, edited by H. A. Hoffner, 81–90. Neukirchen: Butzon & Bercker. [Crimes and Delicts]

Horowitz, Wayne, Takayoshi Oshima, and Seth Sanders. 2006. *Cuneiform in Canaan: Cuneiform Sources from the Land of Israel in Ancient Times*. Jerusalem: Israel Exploration Society. [Sources]

Horst, Friedrich. 1961. *Gottes Recht: Gesammelte Studien zum Recht im Alten Testament*, edited by H. W. Wolff. Munich: Kaiser. [Sources]

Houtman, Cornelis. 1996. "Eine schwangere Frau als Opfer eines Handgemenges (Exodus 21:22–25): Ein Fall von stellvertretender Talion im Bundesbuch?" In *Studies in the Book of Exodus: Redaction–Reception–Interpretation*, edited by M. Vervenne, 381–97. Leuven: Peeters. [Crimes and Delicts]

Hudson, Michael, and Mark Van de Mieroop, eds. 2002. *Debt and Economic Renewal in the Ancient Near East*. Bethesda, MD: CDL Press. [Contracts]

Hugenberger, Gordon P. 1994. *Marriage as a Covenant: A Study of Biblical Law and Ethics Governing Marriage, Developed from the Perspective of Malachi*. Supplements to Vetus Testamentum 52. Leiden: Brill. [Family; Marriage]

Jackson, Bernard S. 1972. *Theft in Early Jewish Law*. Oxford: Oxford University Press. [Crimes and Delicts]

———. 1975. *Essays in Jewish and Comparative Legal History*. Leiden: Brill. [Sources; Family; Crimes and Delects]

———. 1988. "Biblical Laws of Slavery: A Comparative Approach." In *Slavery and Other Forms of Unfree Labour*, edited by L. S. Archer, 86–89. London: Routledge. [Status; Slavery]

———. 2000. *Studies in the Semiotics of Biblical Law*. Journal for the Study of the Old Testament Supplement 314. Sheffield: Sheffield Academic Press. [Sources]

———. 2006a. "Homicide in the Hebrew Bible: A Review Essay." *Zeitschrift für altorientalische und biblische Rechtsgeschichte* 12:362–74. [Crimes and Delicts]

———. 2006b. *Wisdom Laws: A Study of the Mishpatim of Exodus 21:1–22:16*. Oxford: Oxford University Press. [Sources]

Jacobsen, Thorkild. 1970. "An Ancient Mesopotamian Trial for Homicide." In *Toward the Image of Tammuz and Other Essays on Mesopotamian History and Culture*, edited by W. L. Moran, 193–214. Harvard Semitic Studies 21. Cambridge, MA: Harvard University Press. [Litigation]

Kalluveettil, Paul. 1982. *Declaration and Covenant: A Comprehensive Review of Covenant Formulae from the Old Testament and the Ancient Near East*. Analecta Biblica 88. Rome: Biblical Institute Press. [Sources]

Kaufman, Stephen A. 1978. "The Structure of the Deuteronomic Law." *Maarav* 1:105–58. [Sources]

Kitz, Anne Marie. 2000. "Undivided Inheritance and Lot Casting in the Book of Joshua." *Journal of Biblical Literature* 119:601–18. [Inheritance]

Kraeling, Emil. 1953. *The Brooklyn Museum Aramaic Papyri*. New Haven, CT: Yale University Press. [Sources]

Kraus, Fritz R. 1984. *Königliche Verfügungen in altbabylonischer Zeit*. Studia et documenta ad iura Orientis antiqui pertinentia 11. Leiden: Brill. [Sources; Social Justice]

Lafont, Sophie. 1994. "Ancient Near Eastern Laws: Continuity and Pluralism." In *Theory and Method in Biblical and Cuneiform Law: Revision, Interpolation and Development*, edited by B. M. Levinson, 91–118. Journal for the Study of the Old Testament Supplement 181. Sheffield: Sheffield Academic Press. Reprinted 2006; see under Levinson, Bernard M. [Sources; Crimes and Delicts]

———. 1997. "La procédure par serment au Proche-Orient ancien." In *Jurer et maudire: Pratiques politiques et usages juridiques du serment dans le Proche-Orient ancien*, edited by S. Lafont, 185–98. Paris: L'Harmattan. [Litigation]

———. 1999. *Femmes, Droit et Justice dans l'Antiquité orientale: Contribution à l'étude du droit pénal au Proche-Orient ancien*. Orbis Biblicus et Orientalis 165. Göttingen: Vandenhoeck & Ruprecht. [Sources; Family; Crimes and Delicts]

Lemche, Niels Peter. 1975. "The 'Hebrew Slave': Comments on the Slave Law, Exodus 21:2–11." *Vetus Testamentum* 25:129–44. [Status; Slavery]

———. 1976. "Manumission of Slaves—the Fallow Year—the Sabbatical Year—the Jobel Year (Exodus 21:2f., 23:10–11; Deuteronomy 15:10–18; Leviticus 25; Jeremiah 34:8–20; Nehemiah)." *Vetus Testamentum* 26:38–59. [Status; Slavery; Contracts]

———. 1995. "Justice in Western Asia in Antiquity, or: Why No Laws Were Needed!" *Chicago-Kent Law Review* 70:1695–1716. [Sources]

Levine, Etan. 1999. "On Exodus 21:10: *'Onah* and Biblical Marriage." *Zeitschrift für altorientalische und biblische Rechtsgeschichte* 5:133–64. [Family; Contracts]

Levinson, Bernard M., ed. 1994. *Theory and Method in Biblical and Cuneiform Law: Revision, Interpolation and Development*. Journal for the Study of the Old Testament Supplement 181. Sheffield: Sheffield Academic Press. Reprinted under same title. Sheffield: Sheffield Phoenix Press, 2006. [Sources]

———. 1995. "'But You Shall Surely Kill Him!' The Text-Critical and Neo-Assyrian Evidence for MT Deuteronomy 13:10." In *Bundesdokument und Gesetz: Studien zum Deuteronomium*, edited by G. Braulik, 37–63. Herders Biblische Studien 4. Freiburg: Herder. [Sources; Crimes and Delicts]

———. 1997. *Deuteronomy and the Hermeneutics of Legal Innovation*. New York: Oxford University Press. [Sources; Litigation]

———. 2008. *"The Right Chorale": Studies in Biblical Law and Interpretation*. Forschungen zum Alten Testament 54. Tübingen: Mohr Siebeck. [Sources; Crimes and Delicts]

Lewy, Julius. 1958. "The Biblical Institution of *deror* in the Light of Accadian Documents." *Eretz-Israel* 5:21–31. [Contracts; Social Justice]

Lippert, Sandra. 2008. *Einführung in die altägyptische Rechtsgeschichte*. Einführungen und Quellentexte zur Ägyptologie 5. Münster: LIT-Verlag. [Sources]

Locher, Clemens. 1986. *Die Ehre einer Frau in Israel: Exegetische und rechtsvergleichende Studien zu Deuteronomium 22:13–21*. Orbis Biblicus et Orientalis 70. Göttingen: Vandenhoeck & Ruprecht. [Crimes and Delicts]

Loewenstamm, Samuel E. 1980. "The Law of Adultery and the Law of Murder in Biblical and Mesopotamian Law." In *Comparative Studies in Biblical and Ancient*

Oriental Literatures, 146–53. Alter Orient und Altes Testament 204. Kevelaer: Butzon & Bercker. [Crimes and Delicts]

Mabee, Charles. 1980. "Jacob and Laban: The Structure of Judicial Proceedings (Genesis 31:25–42)." *Vetus Testamentum* 30:192–207. [Litigation]

Machinist, Peter. 1998. "Job's Daughters and Their Inheritance in the Testament of Job and Its Biblical Congeners." In *The Echoes of Many Texts—Reflections on Jewish and Christian Traditions: Essays in Honor of Lou H. Silberman*, edited by W. G. Dever and J. E. Wright, 67–80. Brown Judaic Studies 313. Atlanta: Scholars Press. [Inheritance]

Magdalene, F. Rachel. 2004. "Who Is Job's Redeemer? Job 19:25 in Light of Neo-Babylonian Law." *Zeitschrift für altorientalische und biblische Rechtsgeschichte* 10:292–316. [Litigation]

———. 2007. *On the Scales of Righteousness: Neo-Babylonian Trial Law and the Book of Job*. Brown Judaic Studies 348. Providence, RI: Brown Judaic Studies. [Litigation]

Maloney, Robert P. 1974. "Usury and Restrictions on Interest-Taking in the Ancient Near East." *Catholic Biblical Quarterly* 36:1–20. [Contracts]

Malul, Meir. 1989. "Susapinnu." *Journal of the Economic and Social History of the Orient* 32:241–78. [Family; Marriage]

———. 1990a. "Adoption of Foundlings in the Bible and Mesopotamian Documents: A Study of Some Legal Metaphors in Ezekiel 16.1–7." *Journal for the Study of the Old Testament* 46:97–126. [Family]

———. 1990b. *The Comparative Method in Ancient Near Eastern and Biblical Legal Studies*. Alter Orient und Altes Testament 227. Kevelaer: Butzon & Bercker. [Sources]

———. 2007. "What Is the Relationship between Piercing a Slave's Ear (Ex. 21:6) and Circumsizing Him within the Passover Sacrifice (Ex. 12:43–50)?" *Zeitschrift für altorientalische und biblische Rechtsgeschichte* 13:135–58. [Status; Slavery]

Matthews, Victor H. 1987. "Entrance Ways and Threshing Floors: Legally Significant Sites in the Ancient Near East." *Fides et Historia* 19:25–40. [Litigation]

———. 1994. "The Anthropology of Slavery in the Covenant Code." In *Theory and Method in Biblical and Cuneiform Law: Revision, Interpolation and Development*, edited by B. M. Levinson, 119–35. Journal for the Study of the Old Testament Supplement 181. Sheffield: Sheffield Academic Press. Reprinted 2006; see under Levinson, Bernard M. [Status; Slavery]

McCarter, P. Kyle., Jr. 1973. "The River Ordeal in Israelite Literature." *Harvard Theological Review* 66:403–12. [Litigation]

McDowell, Andrea G. 1990. *Jurisdiction in the Workmen's Community of Deir El-Medîna*. Egyptologische Uitgaven 5. Leiden: Nederlands Instituut Voor Het Nabije Oosten. [Litigation]

McKane, William. 1980. "Poison, Trial by Ordeal and the Cup of Wrath." *Vetus Testamentum* 30:474–92. [Litigation]

McKeating, Henry. 1975. "The Development of the Law on Homicide in Ancient Israel." *Vetus Testamentum* 25:46–68. [Crimes and Delicts]

———. 1979. "Sanctions against Adultery in Ancient Israelite Society, with Some Reflections on Methodology in the Study of Old Testament Ethics." *Journal for the Study of the Old Testament* 11:57–72. [Crimes and Delicts]

McKenzie, Donald A. 1964. "Judicial Procedure at the Town Gate." *Vetus Testamentum* 14:100–104. [Litigation]

Meacham, Tirzah. 1997. "The Missing Daughter: Leviticus 18 and 20." *Zeitschrift für die alttestamentliche Wissenschaft* 109:254–59. [Family; Crimes and Delicts]

Meissner, Bruno. 1893. *Beiträge zum altbabylonischen Privatrecht*. Assyriologische Bibliothek 11. Leipzig: Hinrichs. [Sources]

Mendelsohn, Isaac. 1954. "The Disinheritance of Jephthah in the Light of Paragraph 27 of the Lipit-Ishtar Code (Judges 11:1–2)." *Israel Exploration Journal* 4:116–19. [Inheritance]

Mendenhall, George E. 1954. "Law and Covenant in Israel and the Ancient Near East." *Biblical Archaeologist* 17:26–46, 49–76. [Sources]

Michel, Cécile, and Paul Garelli. 1997. *Tablettes paléo-assyriennes de Kültepe*. Paris: De Boccard. [Sources]

Milgrom, Jacob. 2000. *Leviticus 17–22: A New Translation with Introduction and Commentary*. Anchor Bible 3A. New York: Doubleday. [Crimes and Delicts]

Miller, Geoffrey P. 1993. "Contracts of Genesis." *Journal of Legal Studies* 22:15–45. [Contracts]

Miller, James E. 2000. "Sexual Offenses in Genesis." *Journal for the Study of the Old Testament* 90:41–53. [Crimes and Delicts]

Muffs, Yochanan. 2003. *Studies in the Aramaic Legal Papyri from Elephantine*. Handbuch der Orientalistik 66. Leiden: Brill. [Sources]

Neufeld, Edward. 1962. "The Inalienability of Mobile and Immobile Pledges in the Laws of the Bible." *Revue Internationale des Droits de l'Antiquité* 9:33–44. [Contracts]

Nougayrol, Jean. 1955. *Le Palais royal d'Ugarit, III: Textes accadiens et hourrites des archives est, ouest et centrales*. Mission de Ras Shamra 9. Paris: Imprimerie Nationale. [Sources]

Olyan, Saul M. 1994. "'And with a Male You Shall Not Lie the Lying Down of a Woman': On the Meaning and Significance of Leviticus 18:22 and 20:13." *Journal of the History of Sexuality* 5:179–206. [Crimes and Delicts]

Otto, Eckart. 1988a. "Die rechtsgeschichtliche Entwicklung des Depositenrechts in altorientalischen und altisraelitischen Rechtskorpora." *Zeitschrift der Savigny-Stiftung für Rechtsgeschichte* (Romanistische Abteilung) 105:1–31. [Contracts]

———. 1988b. *Wandel der Rechtsbegründungen in der Gesellschaftsgeschichte des Antiken Israel*. Studia Biblica 3. Leiden: Brill. [Sources]

———. 1991a. "Die Geschichte der Talion im Alten Orient und Israel." In *Ernten, was man sät: Festschrift für Klaus Koch zu seinem 65. Geburtstag*, edited by D. R. Daniels, U. Gleßmer, and M. Rösel, 101–30. Neukirchen: Neukirchner Verlag. [Crimes and Delicts]

———. 1991b. *Körperverletzungen in den Keilschriftrechten und im Alten Testament*. Alter Orient und Altes Testament 226. Kevelaer: Butzon & Bercker. [Crimes and Delicts]

———. 1993. "Das Verbot der Wiederherstellung einer geschiedenen Ehe." *Ugarit Forschungen* 24:301–10. [Family]

———. 1996. "The Pre-exilic Deuteronomy as a Revision of the Covenant Code." In *Kontinuum und Proprium: Studien zur Sozial- und Rechtsgeschichte des Alten Orients und des Alten Testaments*, 112–22. Orientalia Biblica et Christiana 8. Wiesbaden: Harrassowitz. [Sources]

———. 2003a. "Recht im antiken Israel." In *Die Rechtskulturen der Antike: Vom Alten Orient bis zum Römischen Reich*, edited by U. Manthe, 151–90. Munich: Beck. [Sources; Crimes and Delicts]

———. 2003b. "Tendenzen der Geschichte des Rechts in der Hebräischen Bibel." *Zeitschrift für altorientalische und biblische Rechtsgeschichte* 9:1–55. [Sources]

———. 2007. "The Pivotal Meaning of Pentateuch Research for a History of Israelite and Jewish Religion and Society." In *South African Perspectives on the Pentateuch between Synchrony and Diachrony*, edited by J. le Roux and E. Otto, 29–53. New York: T. & T. Clark. [Sources]

Paradise, Jonathan S. 1987. "Daughters as 'Sons' at Nuzi." In *Studies on the Civilization and Culture of Nuzi and the Hurrians*, vol. 2, edited by D. Owen and M. Morrison, 203–13. Winona Lake, IN: Eisenbrauns. [Inheritance]

Pardee, Dennis. 1982. *Handbook of Ancient Hebrew Letters: A Study Edition*. Society of Biblical Literature Sources for Biblical Study 15. Chico, CA: Scholars Press. [Sources]

Patrick, Dale. 1985. *Old Testament Law*. Atlanta: John Knox Press. [Sources; General Reference]

———. 1989. "Studying Biblical Law as a Humanities." *Semeia* 45:27–47. [Sources]

Paul, Shalom M. 1970. *Studies in the Book of the Covenant in the Light of Cuneiform and Biblical Law*. Supplements to Vetus Testamentum 18. Leiden: Brill. [Sources]

———. 1979–80. "Adoption Formulae: A Study of Cuneiform and Biblical Legal Clauses." *Journal of Northwest Semitic Languages* 2:173–85. [Family]

Petschow, Herbert. 1965. "Die neubabylonische Zwiegesprächsurkunde und Gen. 23." *Journal of Cuneiform Studies* 19:103–20. [Contracts]

Pfeiffer, Robert H. 1932. *Excavations at Nuzi II: The Archives of Shilwateshup, Son of the King*. Harvard Semitic Series 9. Cambridge, MA: Harvard University Press. [Sources]

Phillips, Anthony. 1970. *Ancient Israel's Criminal Law: A New Approach to the Decalogue*. Oxford: Blackwell. [Crimes and Delicts]

———. 1973. "Some Aspects of Family Law in Pre-exilic Israel." *Vetus Testamentum* 23:349–61. [Family]

———. 1981. "Another Look at Adultery." *Journal of the Society for the Study of the Old Testament* 20:3–25. [Crimes and Delicts]

———. 1984. "The Laws of Slavery: Exodus 21.2–11." *Journal for the Study of the Old Testament* 30:51–66. Reprinted in *Essays on Biblical Law*. Journal for the Study of the Old Testament Supplement 344. Sheffield: Sheffield Academic Press, 2002. [Status; Slavery]

———. 1985. "The Undetectable Offender and the Priestly Legislators." *Journal of Theological Studies* 36:146–50. [Litigation; Crimes and Delicts]

Porten, Bezalel, and Ada Yardeni, eds. 1989. *Textbook of Aramaic Documents from Ancient Egypt*. Vol. 2: *Contracts*. Jerusalem: Hebrew University, and Winona Lake, IN: Eisenbrauns. [Sources]

Porter, Joshua R. 1965. "Legal Aspects of 'Corporate Personality' in the Old Testament." *Vetus Testamentum* 15:361–80. [Sources; Crimes and Delicts]

Postgate, J. N. 1975. "Some Old Babylonian Shepherds and Their Flocks." *Journal of Semitic Studies* 20:1–21. [Contracts]

Pressler, Carolyn. 1993. *The View of Women Found in the Deuteronomic Family Laws*. Beihefte zur Zeitschrift für die alttestamentliche Wissenschaft 216. Berlin: de Gruyter. [Family; Crimes and Delicts]

———. 1998. "Wives and Daughters, Bond and Free." In *Gender and Law in the Hebrew Bible and the Ancient Near East*, edited by V. H. Matthews, B. M. Levinson, and T. Frymer-Kensky, 147–72. Journal for the Study of the Old Testament Supplement 262. Sheffield: Sheffield Academic Press. [Status; Family; Contracts]

Rabinowicz, J. J. 1953. "Marriage Contracts in Ancient Egypt in the Light of Jewish Sources." *Harvard Theological Review* 46:91–97. [Marriage]

Rofé, Alexander. 1986. "The History of the Cities of Refuge in Biblical Law." In *Studies in Scripture*, edited by S. Japhet, 205–23. *Scripta Hierosolymitana* 31. Jerusalem: Magnes. [Crimes and Delicts]

———. 1987. "Family and Sex Laws in Deuteronomy and the Book of the Covenant." *Henoch* 9:131–60. [Family; Crimes and Delicts]

Rogerson, John W. 1970. "The Hebrew Conception of Corporate Personality: A Reexamination." *Journal of Theological Studies* 21:1–16. Reprinted in *Anthropological Approaches to the Old Testament*, edited by B. Lang, 43–59. Philadelphia: Fortress, 1985. [Sources; Crimes and Delicts]

Rollston, Christopher A. 2003. "Non-Provenanced Epigraphs I: Pillaged Antiquities, Northwest Semitic Forgeries, and Protocols for Laboratory Tests." *Maarav* 10:135–93. [Sources]

Roth, Martha T. 1997. *Law Collections from Mesopotamia and Asia Minor*. 2d ed. Society of Biblical Literature Writings from the Ancient World 6. Atlanta: Scholars Press. [Sources]

———. 1998. "Gender and Law: A Case Study from Ancient Mesopotamia." In *Gender and Law in the Hebrew Bible and the Ancient Near East*, edited by V. H. Matthews, B. M. Levinson, and T. Frymer-Kensky, 173–84. Journal for the Study of the Old Testament Supplement 262. Sheffield: Sheffield Academic Press. [Family; Crimes and Delicts]

Rothenbusch, Ralf. 2000. *Die kasuistische Rechtssammlung im "Bundesbuch" (Ex 21,2–11.18–22,16) und ihr literarischer Kontext im Licht altorientalischer Parallelen*. Alter Orient und Altes Testament 259. Münster: Ugarit-Verlag. [Sources; Status; Crimes and Delicts]

San Nicolò, Mariano. 1951. *Babylonische Rechtsurkunden des ausgehenden 8. und des 7. Jahrhunderts v. Chr.* 2 vols. Abhandlungen der Bayerischen Akademie der Wissenschaften 34. Munich: Beck. [Sources]

Sasson, Jack M. 1972. "Numbers 5 and the 'Waters of Judgment.'" *Biblische Zeitschrift*, n.s., 16:249–51. [Litigation]

———, ed. 1995. *Civilizations of the Ancient Near East*. 4 vols. New York: Scribner. [General Reference]

Scheil, Vincent. 1930. *Actes juridiques susiens*. Mémoires de la Mission archéologique de Perse 22. Paris: Librairie Ernest Leroux. [Sources]

Schuler, E. von. 1957. *Hethitische Dienstanweisungen für höhere Hof- und Staatsbeamte*. Graz: Weidner. [Sources]

Schwienhorst-Schönberger, Ludger. 1990. *Das Bundesbuch (Ex 20, 22–23,33): Studien zu seiner Entstehung und Theologie*. Beihefte zur Zeitschrift für die alttestamentliche Wissenschaft 188. Berlin: de Gruyter. [Sources]

Ska, Jean Louis. 2006. *Introduction to Reading the Pentateuch*. Translated by P. Dominique. Winona Lake, IN: Eisenbrauns. [Sources]

Simon, Uriel. 1967. "The Poor Man's Ewe-Lamb, an Example of a Juridical Parable." *Biblica* 48:207–42. [Crimes and Delicts; Contracts]

Stackert, Jeffrey R. 2007. *Rewriting the Torah: Literary Revision in Deuteronomy and the Holiness Legislation*. Forschungen zum alten Testament 52. Tübingen: Mohr Siebeck. [Sources; Crimes and Delicts]

Stewart, David Tabb. 2000. "Ancient Sexual Laws: Text and Intertext of the Biblical Holiness Code and Hittite Law." PhD diss., University of California, Berkeley. [Crimes and Delicts]

Strassmaier, Johann M. 1890. *Inschriften von Cyrus, König von Babylon (538–529 v. Chr.)*. Babylonische Texte 7. Leipzig: Eduard Pfeiffer. [Sources]

Stroud, Ronald S. 1968. *Drakon's Law on Homicide*. Berkeley: University of California Press. [Sources]

Szlechter, Emile. 1958. *Tablettes juridiques de la 1re dynastie de Babylone conservées au Musée d'art et d'histoire de Genève*. Publications de l'Institut de droit romain de l'Université de Paris 16. Paris: Recueil Sirey. [Sources]

Szubin, H. Z., and Bezalel Porten. 2001. "The Status of a Repudiated Spouse: A New Interpretation of Kraeling 7 (TAD B3.8)." *Israel Law Review* 35:46–78. [Family; Inheritance]

Thompson, Thomas, and Dorothy Thompson. 1968. "Some Legal Problems in the Book of Ruth." *Vetus Testamentum* 18:79–99. [Family; Inheritance]

Tsukimoto, Akio. 1988. "Sieben spätbronzezeitliche Urkunden aus Syrien." *Acta Sumerologica* 10:153–89. [Sources]

Tucker, Gene M. 1966a. "The Legal Background of Genesis 23." *Journal of Biblical Literature* 85:77–84. [Contracts]

———. 1966b. "Witness and 'Dates' in Israelite Contracts." *Catholic Biblical Quarterly* 28:42–45. [Litigation; Contracts]

Van Houten, Christiana de Groot. 1991. *The Alien in Israelite Law*. Journal for the Study of the Old Testament Supplement 107. Sheffield: Sheffield Academic Press. [Social Justice]

Van Selms, Adrianus. 1950. "The Best Man and Bride from Sumer to St. John." *Journal of Near Eastern Studies* 9:65–75. [Family]

Van Seters, John. 1996. "The Law of the Hebrew Slave." *Zeitschrift für die alttestamentliche Wissenschaft* 108:534–46. [Status; Slavery; Contracts]

———. 2003. *A Law Book for the Diaspora*. New York: Oxford University Press. [Sources]

Viberg, Åke. 1992. *Symbols of Law: A Contextual Analysis of Legal Symbolic Acts in the Old Testament*. Coniectanea Biblica (Old Testament) 34. Stockholm: Almqvist & Wiksell. [Litigation; Family; Contracts]

Wagenaar, Jan A. 2000. "A Woman Who Practices Sorcery Shall Not Sustain Her Soul: A Note on the Text and Interpretation of Exodus 22:17." *Zeitschrift für altorientalische und biblische Rechtsgeschichte* 6:186–89. [Crimes and Delicts]

———. 2004. "The Annulment of a 'Purchase' Marriage in Exodus 21:7–11." *Zeitschrift für altorientalische und biblische Rechtsgeschichte* 10:219–31. [Status; Family; Contracts]

Washington, Harold C. 1998. "'Lest He Die in Battle and Another Man Take Her': Violence and the Construction of Gender in the Laws of Deuteronomy 20–22." In *Gender and Law in the Hebrew Bible and the Ancient Near East*, edited by V. H. Matthews, B. M. Levinson, and T. Frymer-Kensky, 185–213. Journal for the Study of the Old Testament Supplement 262. Sheffield: Sheffield Academic Press. [Status; Family; Crimes and Delicts]

Watts, James W. 1999. *Reading Law: The Rhetorical Shaping of the Pentateuch*. The Biblical Seminar 59. Sheffield: Sheffield Academic Press. [Sources]

Weinfeld, Moshe. 1990. "The Uniqueness of the Decalogue and Its Place in Jewish Tradition." In *The Ten Commandments in History and Tradition*, edited by B. Segal and G. Levi, 1–44. Jerusalem: Magnes. [Sources]

Weingreen, Jacob. 1966a. "The Case of the Daughters of Zelophehad." *Vetus Testamentum* 16:518–22. [Inheritance]

———. 1966b. "The Case of the Woodgatherer (Numbers 15:32–36)." *Vetus Testamentum* 16:361–64. [Crimes and Delicts]

———. 1972. "The Case of the Blasphemer." *Vetus Testamentum* 22:118–23. [Crimes and Delicts]

Welch, John W. 1990. "Chiasmus in Biblical Law: An Approach to the Structure of Legal Texts in the Bible." In *Jewish Law Association Studies IV: The Boston Conference Volume*, edited by B. S. Jackson and S. M. Passamaneck, 5–22. Atlanta: Scholars Press. [Sources]

———. 2005. *Biblical Law Cumulative Bibliography*. CD-ROM. Provo, UT: Brigham Young University Press, and Winona Lake, IN: Eisenbrauns.

Wells, Bruce. 2004. *The Law of Testimony in the Pentateuchal Codes*. Beihefte zur Zeitschrift für altorientalische und biblische Rechtsgeschichte 4. Wiesbaden: Harrassowitz. [Litigation]

———. 2005. "Sex, Lies, and Virginal Rape: The Slandered Bride and False Accusation in Deuteronomy." *Journal of Biblical Literature* 124:41–72. [Family; Crimes and Delicts]

———. 2006. "The Covenant Code and Near Eastern Legal Traditions: A Response to David P. Wright." *Maarav* 13:85–118. [Sources]

———. 2008. "What Is Biblical Law? A Look at Pentateuchal Rules and Near Eastern Practice." *Catholic Biblical Quarterly* 70:223–43. [Sources]

Wenham, Gordon J. 1972. "*Betulah*, a Girl of Marriageable Age." *Vetus Testamentum* 22:326–48. [Family; Marriage]

———. 1979. "The Restoration of Marriage Reconsidered." *Journal of Jewish Studies* 30:36–40. [Family; Marriage]

———. 1997. "The Gap between Law and Ethics in the Bible." *Journal of Jewish Studies*, 17–29. [Sources; Crimes and Delicts]

Westbrook, Raymond. 1986a. "Lex Talionis and Exodus 21:22–25." *Revue Biblique* 93:52–69. [Crimes and Delicts]

———. 1986b. "The Prohibition on Restoration of Marriage in Deuteronomy 24:1–4." In *Studies in Bible*, edited by S. Japhet, 387–405; Scripta Hierosolymitana 31. Jerusalem: Magnes. [Family; Marriage]

———. 1988. *Studies in Biblical and Cuneiform Law*. Paris: Gabalda. [Sources; Crimes and Delicts; Contracts]

———. 1990. "Adultery in Ancient Near Eastern Law." *Revue Biblique* 97:542–80. [Crimes and Delicts]

———. 1991. *Property and the Family in Biblical Law*. Journal for the Study of the Old Testament Supplement 113. Sheffield: Sheffield Academic Press. [Family; Property and Inheritance]

———. 1994a. "The Deposit Law of Exodus 22:6–12." *Zeitschrift für die alttestamentliche Wissenschaft* 106:390–403. [Contracts]

———. 1994b. "What Is the Covenant Code?" In *Theory and Method in Biblical and Cuneiform Law: Revision, Interpolation and Development*, edited by B. M. Levinson, 13–34. Journal for the Study of the Old Testament Supplement 181. Sheffield: Sheffield Academic Press. Reprinted 2006; see under Levinson, Bernard M. [Sources]

———. 1995a. "Riddles in Deuteronomic Law." In *Bundesdokument und Gesetz: Studien zum Deuteronomium*, edited by G. Braulik, 159–74. Herders Biblische Studien 4. Freiburg: Herder. [Sources]

———. 1995b. "Slave and Master in Ancient Near Eastern Law." *Chicago-Kent Law Review* 70:1631–76. [Status; Slavery; Contracts]

———. 1996. "Biblical Law." In *An Introduction to the History and Sources of Jewish Law*, edited by N. S. Hecht, B. S. Jackson, and S. M. Passamaneck, 1–17. Oxford: Oxford University Press. [Sources]

———. 1998. "The Female Slave." In *Gender and Law in the Hebrew Bible and the Ancient Near East*, edited by V. H. Matthews, B. M. Levinson, and T. Frymer-Kensky, 214–38. Journal for the Study of the Old Testament Supplement 262. Sheffield: Sheffield Academic Press. [Status; Slavery; Contracts]

———. 2000. "Codification and Canonization." In *La Codification des lois dans l'antiquité: Actes du Colloque de Strasbourg, 27–29 Novembre 1997*, edited by E. Lévy, 33–47. Travaux du Centre de Recherche sur le Proche-Orient et la Grèce antiques 16. Paris: De Boccard. [Sources]

———, ed. 2003. *A History of Ancient Near Eastern Law*. 2 vols. Handbuch der Orientalistik 72. Leiden: Brill. [General Reference]

———. 2006. "Reflections on the Law of Homicide in the Ancient World." *Maarav* 13:143–71. [Crimes and Delicts]

———. 2007. "The Trial of Jeremiah." In *Reading the Law: Studies in Honour of Gordon J. Wenham*, edited by J. G. McConville and K. Möller, 95–107. New York: T. & T. Clark. [Litigation]

———. 2008. "The Laws of Biblical Israel." In *The Hebrew Bible: New Insights and Scholarship*, edited by F. Greenspahn, 99–119. New York: New York University Press. [Sources]

Westbrook, Raymond, and Richard Jasnow, eds. 2001. *Security for Debt in Ancient Near Eastern Law*. Culture and History of the Ancient Near East 9. Leiden: Brill. [Contracts]

Westbrook, Raymond, and Roger Woodard. 1990. "The Edict of Tudhaliya IV." *Journal of the American Oriental Society* 110:641–59.

Willetts, R. F. 1967. *The Law Code of Gortyn*. Kadmos Supplement 1. Berlin: de Gruyter. [Sources]

Willis, Timothy M. 2001. *The Elders of the City: A Study of the Elders-Laws in Deuteronomy*. Society of Biblical Literature Monograph 55. Atlanta: Society of Biblical Literature. [Family; Crimes and Delicts]

Wilson, Robert R. 1980. "Israel's Judicial System in the Preexilic Period." *Jewish Quarterly Review* 74:229–48. [Litigation]

———. 1993. "The Role of Law in Early Israelite Society." In *Law, Politics and Society in the Ancient Mediterranean World*, edited by B. Halpern and D. W. Hobson, 90–99. Sheffield: Sheffield Academic Press. [Sources]

Wright, David P. 2003. "The Laws of Hammurabi as a Source for the Covenant Collection (Exodus 20:23–23:19)." *Maarav* 10:11–87. [Sources]

———. 2004. "The Compositional Logic of the Goring Ox and Negligence Laws in the Covenant Collection (Ex 21:28–36)." *Zeitschrift für altorientalische und biblische Rechtsgeschichte* 10:93–142. [Sources]

Yadin, Yigael. 1962. "Expedition D: The Cave of Letters." *Israel Exploration Journal* 12:235–37. [Sources]

Yaron, Reuven. 1957. "On Divorce in Old Testament Times." *Revue Internationale des Droits de l'Antiquité* 4:117–28. [Family; Marriage]

———. 1959. "Redemption of Persons in the Ancient Near East." *Revue Internationale des Droits de l'Antiquité* 6:155–76. [Contracts]

———. 1962. *Introduction to the Law of the Aramaic Papyri*. Oxford: Clarendon. [Sources; Family]

———. 1963. "Duobus sororibus coniunctio, Leviticus 18:18." *Revue Internationale des Droits de l'Antiquité* 10:115–36. [Family; Crimes and Delicts]

———. 1966. "The Restoration of Marriage." *Journal of Jewish Studies* 17:1–11. [Family; Marriage]

———. 2004. "Drei Deuteronomische Gesetze." *Zeitschrift für altorientalische und biblische Rechtsgeschichte* 10:195–206. [Family; Crimes and Delicts; Contracts]

Zulueta, Francis de, ed. 1951. *The Institutes of Gaius*. Vol. 1: *Text with Critical Notes and Translation*. Oxford: Clarendon, 1951.

Index